Steph

SUSAN
SAYERS

Gathered for Prayer

100 Thematic Intercessions

First published in 1996 by
KEVIN MAYHEW LTD
Rattlesden
Bury St Edmunds
Suffolk IP30 0SZ

ISBN   0 86209 853 X
Catalogue No 1500057

Cover design by Angela Staley
Edited by Michael Forster
Typesetting by Louise Hill
Printed and bound in Great Britain

Contents

WORSHIP, DISCIPLESHIP, MISSION

Foreword

Christians are gathering to pray together somewhere in the world all the time. Our planet is surrounded by an unbroken, constant circle of prayer which opens up channels for God to work through and touches the raw places with peace.

This work of prayer to which we are all called is precious, costly and vital, and those whose ministry it is to lead Christians in prayer carry a great responsibility. We need to provide in our churches the kind of spiritual landscape in which real, fervent prayer can develop and flourish.

Corporate prayer can only be the outward expression of everyone's personal, hidden prayer life, so it is important that people are taught and encouraged and inspired at every stage of their spiritual journey. Praying needs to be visibly undergirding all decision making and planning. In formal worship those leading the prayers need to be well prepared, not just in delivery, but in openness to God's prompting, since God knows and loves each person who is going to be present, and their particular situations.

This book of thematic intercessions provides you with guidelines and suggestions for leading formal prayer, and there are silences for private or open prayer throughout. I have included responses in the intercessions, since many churches find these helpful, but they can easily be omitted if that suits your church's style better.

SUSAN SAYERS

GOD OUR CREATOR AND REDEEMER

We depend on God

Let us pray in humility to God
who creates and sustains all things.

We pray for the Church, the body of Christ;
that regardless of rank or position,
its members may be noticeable
by their unselfish humility,
so that through their good work
God may be glorified.
Silence
Great creator God,
let us show your glory.

We bring before God the world's leaders
and their governments,
and all in influential positions;
that they may make good use
of their power,
and aim to serve
the needs of others.
Silence
Great creator God,
let us show your glory.

We remember the disabled,
the mentally and physically disadvantaged,
and those whose bodies or minds
have been damaged
through accidents or violence;

we commit them to the calm and peace of Christ.

Silence

Great creator God,
let us show your glory.

We pray for those we serve in our daily lives,
and all who serve us;
that we may care for each other
with kindness and friendship,
knowing that we are all
brothers and sisters before God.

Silence

Great creator God,
let us show your glory.

In silence, we pray for our own intentions to God, our
loving Father.

Lord God,
Creator of all things,
we ask you to hear these prayers,
through Jesus Christ our Lord.
Amen.

A world of inequality and indifference

Let us pray to our heavenly Father, who holds all creation in his care.

We pray for the Christian Church;
that it may truly serve the world,
and proclaim God's love
not only by word
but also through action.
Silence

Yours, Lord, is the power:
sufficient for all our needs.

We pray for the world
with its areas of luxury
and deprivation;
that as we become more aware
of the problems,
we may be guided and inspired
to solve them,
and as technology brings us closer,
we may grow in mutual respect
and understanding.
Silence

Yours, Lord, is the power:
sufficient for all our needs.

We ask for an outpouring of God's love
on the unnoticed, the unloved
and those for whom no one cares;
those whose lives
are plagued with poverty and disease;
the homeless and the refugees.
Silence
Yours, Lord, is the power:
sufficient for all our needs.

We remember the families represented here,
and all families of every nationality;
that children may be nurtured
in love and security,
and homes may be places
of peace and joy.
Silence
Yours, Lord, is the power:
sufficient for all our needs.

In silence let us commend
our own particular needs and thankfulness
to the God of power and mercy.

Heavenly Father,
hear these prayers,
through your Son Jesus Christ.
Amen.

Entrust the world to God

Let us pray to God, who has promised to hear us and is always true to his word.

We pray for the world-wide Christian family;
that it may offer hope
to the despairing,
peace to the distressed,
fulfilment to those who seek,
and refreshment to the weary.
Silence

Lord, you are our strength:
we believe and trust in you.

We pray for a shrinking world
and those whose authority can affect it
for good or ill;
that we may all learn
to trust one another
and forgive each other
more readily.
Silence

Lord, you are our strength:
we believe and trust in you.

We bring before their Creator
those who are chronically ill
and in constant pain;
those who are frightened by their illness
and those who are approaching death;

that they may receive the sustaining
peace of Christ,
who knows them personally,
and whose love for them extends
even through death itself.

Silence

Lord, you are our strength:
we believe and trust in you.

We ask God's blessing upon
members of our own families
with their particular needs and difficulties;
on our own lives and spiritual growth;
that we may learn to trust more in God
than in ourselves,
and be alert to his guidance each day.

Silence

Lord, you are our strength:
we believe and trust in you.

We pray in silence to God
who created us and knows our needs.

God our Father,
accept our prayers;
as we learn to trust more in your love,
may we grow to be more like Christ
and reflect the radiance of his love;
through the same Jesus Christ our Lord.
Amen.

Jesus is Lord of heaven and earth

Let us pray in the name of Jesus Christ
in whom is our hope of redemption.

We pray for all those involved
in spreading God's word
of truth and joy;
that their lives may be instruments
by which God's love
is spread through the world.
Silence

Christ, King of Glory:
help us to do your will.

We remember in prayer
the many different cultures and races
which make up Creation;
that we may all learn
from one another,
until God's kingdom
is established on earth.
Silence

Christ, King of Glory:
help us to do your will.

We pray for the casualties of materialistic,
unjust or corrupt society;
that, in the light of Christ,

people may recognise needs
and have the courage to act.

Silence

Christ, King of Glory:
help us to do your will.

We hold in the light of Christ's love
each person here,
and the circle of lives
linked to each one
at home and at work;
that with these immediate contacts
we may open the way for God to act
by becoming channels of his peace
and his redemptive love.

Silence

Christ, King of Glory:
help us to do your will.

We pray in silence, now,
for our own particular needs and concerns.

Father,
accept our prayers;
fit us for heaven,
to live with you for ever,
through Jesus Christ our Lord.
Amen.

God redeems his creation

Full of thanks and praise,
we worship God our Father
for the earth is rich with his blessing;
let us pray to him now.

We pray that the will of God
may be accomplished
in every life and every situation;
that Christians may become
increasingly receptive
and ready to act as channels
of his redeeming grace.
Silence
Father of the living Word:
speak in our hearts.

We pray that the world may be drawn
into a deep, abiding love:
the love of the Father and the Son.
Silence
Father of the living Word:
speak in our hearts.

We hold in our prayers
all those who are physically
or mentally disadvantaged in any way,
and for all who minister to them.
For ourselves, we ask
for greater acceptance of others

who look, speak or behave
differently from ourselves.

Silence

Father of the living Word:
speak in our hearts.

We pray that all of us here present
may become more aware
of the privileges
and responsibilities
of being the children of God.

Silence

Father of the living Word:
speak in our hearts.

Now, in the space of silence,
we bring to God our Father
our own particular prayers.

Silence

Heavenly Father,
we ask this through Jesus Christ our Lord.
Amen.

God gives meaning to creation

Let us remember with gratitude
all that God has done for us;
let us bring to his love
the needs and concerns
of the Church and of the world.
Let us pray.

We bring to his love the daily work
of each member of Christ's body:
that in constant prayer
we may learn God's will
and his way of doing things,
until we work exclusively for his glory.
Silence
Lord, in you we trust:
we look to you for help.

We bring to his love the mistakes,
short-sightedness and arrogance
of our world;
that in Christ we may learn
to respect one another
and the treasures of the planet we inhabit.
Silence
Lord, in you we trust:
we look to you for help.

We bring to his love
the wounded and the afraid,
the despairing and the rejected,
that they may find Christ
suffering alongside them
and allow him to restore them to full life.
Silence

Lord, in you we trust:
we look to you for help.

We bring to his love our busy concern
with unimportant things;
that in spending more time in Christ's company
we may learn to act and react
with the character of Jesus.
Silence

Lord, in you we trust:
we look to you for help.

Now, in silence,
we bring our individual prayers
to our heavenly Father,
who has promised to hear us.
Silence

Almighty Father,
hear the prayers we offer,
and use our bodies, minds and spirits
in establishing your kingdom.
In the name of Jesus we pray.
Amen.

Christ, the hope of creation

In the spirit of Christ,
who has promised he will return,
let us pray together
for the needs of the Church
and of the world.

Let us pray that the Church
and all its members
may never become static
but flow constantly forward
in the direction God wants us to go,
true to Christ's teaching,
in unswerving loyalty to him
and undistracted by worldly values.
Silence
Lord, give us wisdom:
to know and love you more.

Let us pray that we may tend
and care for the world
God has given us;
that its food and riches may be shared
and wisely used,
and its resources safely
and thoughtfully deployed
without waste or destruction.
Silence
Lord, give us wisdom:
to know and love you more.

Let us pray that all those
who are ill, injured or distressed
may be touched
by the healing hand of Jesus
and be made whole,
comforted by his presence.
Silence

Lord, give us wisdom:
to know and love you more.

Let us pray that we may be more watchful,
preparing ourselves more thoroughly
day by day
to meet our Lord
face to face.
Silence

Lord, give us wisdom:
to know and love you more.

In a time of silence,
we share with God our Father
our personal burdens, joys and sorrows.
Silence

Father,
whose character is full
of mercy and compassion,
accept these prayers
for the sake of Jesus our Saviour.
Amen.

God meets our needs

Let us gather together our concerns
and pray to our heavenly Father
who is always ready to listen
and eager to help us.

We pray for the Church,
especially in its work of counselling
and welcoming those in great need or difficulty;
that our Christian witness
may vividly reflect
the generous love of Christ.
Silence

Hear us, heavenly Father:
and let your will be done.

We pray for the world's leaders
and all who hold positions of authority
and responsibility;
that the world's resources may be shared
and fairly distributed,
so that all its inhabitants
have enough for their needs.
Silence

Hear us, heavenly Father:
and let your will be done.

We pray for the starving and malnourished,
and for all who are weakened
by lack of sufficient food;

for all refugees and asylum seekers,
and those whose mental capacity
makes them vulnerable to inadequate provision
of food, clothing or housing.
Silence

Hear us, heavenly Father:
and let your will be done.

We pray for ourselves,
and for those we meet each day;
that we may be more prepared
to give our time,
energy, talents and money
in serving those in need
and working hand in hand with Christ.
Silence

Hear us, heavenly Father:
and let your will be done.

In the silence of our hearts,
we pray to our heavenly Father
about our own particular concerns.
Silence

Father of mercy,
you are always more ready to give
than we are to receive;
in thankfulness we welcome
your Spirit into our lives,
and ask you to accept our prayers,
through Jesus Christ, your Son.
Amen.

The light of God's glory

Let us pray to God,
whose glory is all around us,
with thankful and adoring hearts.

We bring to the Lord
all those involved
with teaching the Christian faith;
our schools and children's ministry,
and missionaries – especially . . .
(any missionary work
connected with or supported by
the particular church)
Silence
Father of Light:
shine in the darkness.

We bring to the Lord
all peoples of our earth
with their different cultures,
philosophies and traditions;
multi-racial communities,
especially those experiencing problems
with mutual understanding and harmony.
Silence
Father of Light:
shine in the darkness.

We bring to the Lord all new-born babies,
especially those who are unwanted
or abandoned;
all people who are elderly
and approaching death,
especially those who are frightened.
Silence
Father of Light:
shine in the darkness.

We bring to the Lord our own local church,
our programme for education and outreach,
our availability to those who do not yet know
the richness of God's love;
its areas of stagnation
and its potential for growth.
Silence
Father of Light:
shine in the darkness.

In silence,
as God the Father listens with love,
we name our own particular cares and concerns.
Silence
Heavenly Father,
we ask you to accept these prayers,
through Christ our Saviour.
Amen.

Chosen and called

As God's chosen people,
his adopted sons and daughters,
let us pray to him now
in the Spirit of Jesus Christ.

We pray for all who are called
to spread the news
of hope and joy for humanity;
that their teaching may be inspired
so as to draw many, through Christ,
to their loving creator.

Silence

Father of Wisdom:
open our eyes to your truth.

We remember all those who are called
to sit on committees;
all decision makers and policy planners,
that they may be guided to work
in accordance with God's will,
so that the world is governed
and ordered wisely.

Silence

Father of Wisdom:
open our eyes to your truth.

We hold before God,
all who work with the sick;
those who are chronically ill,

or suffering from a long-term disability;
that even through intense pain
there may be positive, spiritual growth,
and a deeper awareness of God's presence.
Silence
Father of Wisdom:
open our eyes to your truth.

We pray for those who are called
to care for children,
through fostering, adoption,
or in residential homes;
also for children separated from their families,
for those waiting to be placed
in loving homes,
for a greater sharing of love
and the growth of mutual trust.
Silence
Father of Wisdom:
open our eyes to your truth.

In a time of silence
we share with God our Father
any needs and burdens
known to us personally.
Silence
Almighty Father,
hear our prayers,
and make us alert to your response,
through Jesus Christ our Lord.
Amen.

Christ reigns in glory

Trusting in Christ's victory
over all evil,
let us pray to the Father
for the needs of the Church
and the world.

We pray for all who witness to Christ
in spite of danger and persecutions;
all who work to bring others to Christ,
that in God's strength
they may be blessed and encouraged
and bear much fruit.
Silence
Christ, King of Glory:
reign in our hearts.

Let us remember world leaders
and all diplomats and advisers;
that God's will for the world
may be done.
Silence
Christ, King of Glory:
reign in our hearts.

We bring to the Lord
those who have never received the Good News
of God's saving love;
also places where violence and terrorism
make normal life impossible;

that the Spirit of Jesus,
the Prince of Peace,
may filter through to increase
love and understanding,
respect and goodwill.

Silence

Christ, King of Glory:
reign in our hearts.

We pray for ourselves
and those with whom we live and work;
that in everything we do,
and every minute we live,
God may be glorified
and his will accomplished.

Silence

Christ, King of Glory:
reign in our hearts.

God our Father loves us;
in silence we bring
our own prayers
to him now.

Silence

Father,
trusting in your great love for us,
we bring you these prayers
through Jesus Christ our Lord.
Amen.

Redeemed by Christ's suffering

In gratitude for Christ's
saving death,
let us pray together
to our loving Father.

We pray for all who, in following Christ,
have encountered suffering,
danger or persecution;
that they may be supported and sustained
by the presence of the suffering Christ.
Silence
Heavenly Father:
Your love sets us free.

We pray for the innocent who suffer
as a result of the world's mistakes,
ineptitudes, misplaced priorities or greed;
that love may breach
the walls of prejudice
and bring fresh life
to the deserts of hopelessness.
Silence
Heavenly Father:
Your love sets us free.

We remember the aimless and bewildered;
those who grieve
and those who try to repress their grief;
all who are finding a burden
desperately hard to bear.
Silence
Heavenly Father:
Your love sets us free.

We offer to God
our own friends and loved ones
as well as ourselves;
that we may trust Jesus
to bring good out of every situation,
however hopeless it seems.
Silence
Heavenly Father:
Your love sets us free.

God our Father loves us.
In silence now
we bring our individual prayers to him.
Silence
Father,
in your unfailing mercy,
we ask you to accept these prayers,
through Jesus Christ.
Amen.

GOD WITH US

Jesus, King of Love

As we welcome Jesus,
and hail him as our King,
let us offer to God our Father in prayer
the deep concerns and needs
of the Church and the world.

We bring to his love all who are baptised,
and especially those who have lost their faith
or stopped praying;
that they may be brought back
through Christ's love,
and put into contact with those
who can guide and reassure them.
Silence
Christ, King of Love:
we pledge ourselves to your service.

We bring to his love all gatherings of people:
all meetings, or political demonstrations,
social and sporting events,
that they may be peaceful and ordered,
offering enjoyment, or influencing for good,
rather than inciting to violence and evil.
Silence
Christ, King of Love:
we pledge ourselves to your service.

We bring to his love those suffering
from incurable or life-threatening diseases;

those who are denied necessary medical care;
that we may be ready to use our time,
money and influence,
so that unnecessary suffering and death are avoided.

Silence

Christ, King of Love:
we pledge ourselves to your service.

We bring to his love our own loved ones,
families and friends,
and especially those
from whom we are separated;
people who are missing from their homes
and those who wait for them;
that God's powerful love
may be a protection against all evil.

Silence

Christ, King of Love:
we pledge ourselves to your service.

Knowing that God our Father
hears the cries of his children,
we pray in silence for our own needs and cares.

Silence

Merciful Father,
we know that you hold all life in your hand;
please hear our prayers,
through Jesus our Redeemer.
Amen.

God comes to us with grace

In the knowledge that God our Father
is here present,
let us pray.

We pray for the Church of Christ
and its mission to the world;
that it may be a sign of his presence,
call sinners to repentance
and bring many to the joy of living in your love.
Silence

Lord, our Father:
hear us as we pray.

We pray for the whole created world
and its people;
that no evil may thwart God's will,
but rather that his kingdom
may be established
and his will fulfilled.
Silence

Lord, our Father:
hear us as we pray.

We remember before God
all who suffer
mentally, physically and spiritually;
those who see no further

than immediate physical comforts,
and do not realise their spiritual poverty.
Silence

Lord, our Father:
hear us as we pray.

We hold before God this church
and the surrounding community,
with all who live and work within it;
that we may strive each day
to align ourselves
with the life of Christ,
who saves us from our sin.
Silence

Lord, our Father:
hear us as we pray.

In the silence of God's stillness,
we name any we know
who especially need our prayer.
Silence

Lord, our Father:
hear us as we pray.
Silence

Father,
trusting in your mercy,
we lay these prayers before you,
through Jesus Christ our Lord.
Amen.

Let us glorify God

As one family in Christ,
we come before our heavenly Father
and pray to him now.

We pray for all those Christians
who are persecuted for their faith;
that they may be strengthened
by the assurance of Christ's presence
for all time and in all places.
Silence
Come to us, Father:
our hope and our joy.

We pray for all politicians
and government ministers;
that they may discern Christ's truth
and be given the courage
to walk faithfully in it.
Silence
Come to us, Father:
our hope and our joy.

We bring into the light of God's love
the malnourished and the starving,
all who have become diseased
from contaminated water supplies;
that as fellow human beings
we may be led by the love of Christ
to share the world's resources.

Silence

Come to us, Father:
our hope and our joy.

We remember in prayer our own community,
and especially the many groups
of Christian people;
that Jesus' love and desire for our unity
may inspire us to break down barriers
and build bridges
to the greater glory of God.

Silence

Come to us, Father:
our hope and our joy.

In silence,
we pray to the Lord
for our own intentions.

Silence

Father,
trusting in your love,
we lay these prayers before you
through Jesus Christ our Lord.

Amen.

Share the Good News

As Christ approaches us
with welcoming arms,
let us approach him and pray
in his Spirit
with humility and love.

We pray that Christ will use all Christians,
from the very young to the very old,
in witnessing to the reality
of his presence
by the lives they lead.

Silence

Living Lord:
speak in our hearts.

We pray that, through the wonder and beauty
of God's created world,
many will be alerted
to the sustaining love
of its creator.

Silence

Living Lord:
speak in our hearts.

We remember the worried,
the confused and the anxious;
that in trusting Jesus
and laying their troubles before him,
they may experience the release

and freedom
that his love provides.
Silence
Living Lord:
speak in our hearts.

We pray for ourselves,
our relatives and friends,
that we may live more closely with Christ,
so that we may see him more clearly,
become more like him,
and witness more effectively
to his love.
Silence
Living Lord:
speak in our hearts.

In silence, filled with love,
we name our particular prayer burdens.
Silence
Father,
may we, who confess Christ as Lord,
live in his strength.
Through the same Jesus Christ our Lord.
Amen.

The Lord is our light

Our heavenly Father
guides us faithfully
and enlightens our lives.
Let us pray to him now,
for the Church
and for the world.

We pray that we may be ready
to follow Christ wherever he leads us,
even if the direction is unexpected
or demanding.
Silence
Lord of lords:
hear us, we pray.

We pray that all nations may rejoice
in the light of goodness
and reject the darkness of evil.
Silence
Lord of lords:
hear us, we pray.

We pray that in the brightness of love,
Christ may be revealed
turning the doubtful to faith,
the despairing to hope,
and the revengeful to forgiveness.

Silence

Lord of lords:
hear us, we pray.

We pray that no opportunity may be lost
in sharing the joy and peace of Christ
with those we meet
in our daily lives.

Silence

Lord of lords:
hear us, we pray.

We pray to the Lord in silence,
for our own needs and cares

Silence

Father,
we commend our lives
to your loving care,
through Jesus Christ our Lord.

Amen.

The family of God

As brothers and sisters in Christ,
let us pray to our heavenly Father
for the Church
and for the world.

We ask for grace
that we may open the doors of our homes
to welcome Jesus;
that Christian families
may be an example
and a source of strength,
a ministry of warmth and generosity.
Silence
God our Father:
bless our homes.

We pray that our society may be based
on mutual respect and understanding,
on co-operation and care.
Silence
God our Father:
bless our homes.

We pray for all families who are suffering
through poverty, sickness,
separation or war;
that God's presence
may comfort and strengthen them,
and that we may work in Christ

to ease their burdens
and minister to their needs.
Silence
God our Father:
bless our homes.

We pray for our own families and loved ones,
both living and departed,
both those we feel close to
and those we find difficult
to understand.
Silence
God our Father:
bless our homes.

As members of Christ's family,
we name those we know
who are in any particular need.
Silence
Father,
we ask you to hear our prayers,
through Jesus Christ our Lord.
Amen.

Jesus is here

Let us pray,
with our hearts filled
with thanksgiving,
to the God who loves us
so completely.

We pray that the joy
and wonder of Christ's presence
may infuse our lives,
so that the Good News may be spread
throughout the world.
Silence
Loving Father:
we come to adore.

We pray that all in authority
may be filled with the wisdom
and compassion of God.
Silence
Loving Father:
we come to adore.

We pray that the lonely,
the rejected and the isolated
may have knowledge and confirmation
of God's abiding warmth and love.
Silence
Loving Father:
we come to adore.

We pray that all families may be blessed
with his everlasting joy,
and all homes may be filled
with his peace.

Silence

Loving Father:
we come to adore.

In the silence
of these moments,
we make our particular concerns known to God
our loving Father.

Silence

Father,
accept these prayers:
in wonder and adoration
we offer our lives to you,
with and through
our Lord Jesus Christ.

Amen.

Waiting expectantly

Since we are promised
that Christ will return,
let us pray in hope and expectation.
Let us bring to his healing and love
the needs of the Church
and the world.
Silence

Come, Lord Jesus:
live in us now.

We pray for all Christian people;
for increased love and commitment,
working within the world
as yeast within the dough.
Silence

Come, Lord Jesus:
live in us now.

We pray for those in authority,
that they may base their priorities
and decisions
on the foundations of God's power:
justice and mercy.
Silence

Come, Lord Jesus:
live in us now.

We pray for those who suffer;
for God's strength and support
during pain, grief or distress,
so that their very suffering
may become a channel
for God's redeeming love.
Silence
Come, Lord Jesus:
live in us now.

We pray for the local community,
that God's presence may be known
in the varied, separate lives surrounding us;
that, alerted to their needs,
we may work in Christ to care and provide.
Silence
Come, Lord Jesus:
live in us now.

In the silence of God's stillness
we name any we know
who specially need our prayer.
Silence
Father,
you came to show us the true way to life.
Help us to progress along that way
in your strength,
through Jesus Christ our Lord.
Amen.

Jesus is the Word made flesh

Let us pray to God our Father
because he loves us so dearly.

We pray that the Word who became flesh
may be so manifest in our lives
that other people notice
and are attracted to Jesus
by the way we live and love.
Silence
Lord of the universe:
be known in us today.

We pray that the world may stop
its noise, chatter and arguing
long enough to recognise
the Word of hope and peace.
Silence
Lord of the universe:
be known in us today.

We pray that God will bless and support
all expectant mothers
and those in labour;
and that all new-born babies
and young children
may be cherished, loved
and protected

as they bear God's love
to us anew.
Silence
Lord of the universe:
be known in us today.

We pray that there may be more
understanding and mercy
in our family relationships,
with Christ always among us –
not an occasional visitor.
Silence
Lord of the universe:
be known in us today.

We name in this silence
any known to us
with particular needs and burdens.
Silence
Father,
we can never thank you enough
for coming to save us;
please hear our prayers which we offer
through Jesus, your Son.
Amen.

Guidance and correction

Jesus assures us that
wherever two or three
meet in his name
he will be with them;
in confidence, then,
let us bring to our Father
our needs and cares.

We pray that God's love
will spill out through his Church
to the world,
filling all teaching,
all advice and counsel,
all correction and guidance.
Silence

Father, hear us:
renew us in love.

We pray that God's Spirit
of forgiveness and acceptance
will permeate the social and political
fabric of our world
until we are able to criticise gently,
and accept criticism honestly;
discuss differences calmly,
and be prepared to negotiate rationally.
Silence

Father, hear us:
renew us in love:

We pray that God's comfort and consolation
will soothe those who are afraid
or in great pain,
refresh those who are mentally
or physically exhausted
and be a lifeline to those
who are broken-hearted or in despair.

Silence

Father, hear us:
renew us in love:

We pray that the light of Christ
may shine in our hearts
to show us our faults
and enable us to admit them;
to shine through our lives in
the way we treat each other,
especially when we disagree or feel hurt.

Silence

Father, hear us:
renew us in love:

In silence,
as God our Father listens with love,
we name our own particular cares and concerns.

Silence

Father,
we ask you to gather up
these prayers of your people,
through the merits of Jesus, our Saviour.

Amen.

Do not be afraid

Let us approach our heavenly Father,
acknowledging the wonder
of his involvement with us,
and asking him to help us.

We pray for all who labour
to spread the Good News,
especially those who face
threatening behaviour,
imprisonment or persecution;
for those who are tempted
to remain silent
in order to avoid danger
to themselves or their families;
that they may be given courage
by Christ's promise
to keep them eternally safe.
Silence
Lord, in our weakness:
we ask for your help.

We pray for our world
in all its injustice, cruelty and oppression;
its confused priorities,
its lost opportunities,
its misguided zeal;
that we may be guided unceasingly
by the level-headed,
compassionate leadership
of God's Spirit.

Silence
Lord, in our weakness:
we ask for your help.

We pray for all who are wounded,
injured and in pain;
that they may find Christ
alongside them in their suffering;
we pray for all those who inflict pain on others,
and all who are fired with hatred;
that their lives may be transformed
by encountering Christ,
who loves them.
Silence
Lord, in our weakness:
we ask for your help.

We pray for our families,
friends and neighbours;
for the very young
and the very old in our care;
for wisdom to see opportunities
of showing Christ's love,
and for enough energy and time
to do what God needs us to.
Silence
Lord, in our weakness:
we ask for your help.

Knowing that God loves us
with full understanding,
we offer our private prayers
to him in silence.

Silence

Merciful Father,
protect us during this week
and through our lives,
and hear these prayers
for the sake of Jesus Christ.

Amen.

Unity in diversity

Gathered together
in the love and fellowship
of God the Three in One,
let us speak to the Father
of our needs and cares.

We pray for the work of the Church
in suburbs, cities, slums and villages,
especially where there is
violent opposition,
complacency or apathy,
that people of all traditions
and outlooks
who work with Christ
may be blessed and encouraged
so that many may find peace
in God's love.

Silence

Father, Son and Holy Spirit:
keep us in your love.

We pray for the world,
with its mistakes and misunderstandings,
all the breakdowns in communication
between individuals,
groups or nations,
that the unifying love of God
may draw people together,
helping them to find common ground
on which they can build,
rather than dwelling on hurtful divisions.

Silence
Father, Son and Holy Spirit:
keep us in your love.

We pray for those
who are without homes
or live in crowded,
inadequate accommodation;
those living alone and isolated;
for the hungry and malnourished;
that God's love, working through us, his body,
may reach those in desperate need
and give them new hope.
Silence
Father, Son and Holy Spirit:
keep us in your love.

We pray for a greater love and fellowship
among ourselves in this church
and this community,
and in our families;
that God's life living in us
may make us more ready to listen,
to respond and to forgive,
to put ourselves out
and seek to understand.
Silence
Father, Son and Holy Spirit:
keep us in your love.

Together in silence
we name those known to us
who need our prayers.

Silence

Father almighty,
in the Spirit we pray,
and ask you to hear our prayers,
through Jesus Christ our Lord.

Amen.

62

Christy, always present

In the knowledge of Christ's
constant presence,
let us pray to our heavenly Father,
the God of mercy and love.

We pray for the world-wide
Christian community,
that unceasing prayer and praise
may be offered as our planet turns
through night and day,
that we may be strengthened and encouraged
to reveal Christ to the world.
Silence

Hear us, ever-present God:
we trust in you.

We pray for the direction
and guidance of our world;
that in all areas of discussion, negotiation,
policy-making and reform,
Christ may be present,
touching our lives and wills
with his peace.
Silence

Hear us, ever-present God:
we trust in you.

We pray for all those whose happiness
is less because of war, homelessness,
pain or separation from loved ones;
that in all their troubles they may know
that the humility of Christ's birth,
life and death on this earth
confirms his immense love for us
and his desire to share our suffering.

Silence

Hear us, ever-present God:
we trust in you.

We pray for our homes and families,
that we may recognise Christ's presence,
living among us,
deepening and extending our love
one for another.

Silence

Hear us, ever-present God:
we trust in you.

We pray in silence now
for our own particular needs and concerns.

Silence

Father,
with thanks and joy
we offer these prayers
through Jesus our Saviour.

Amen.

Christ, our ever-present hope

Trusting in the promise of God
that he will never desert us,
let us approach him
with our cares and concerns.

Let us pray for all people
who are imprisoned or persecuted
because of their faith;
for the lapsed and the doubting;
that they may know
the sovereignty of God,
and his presence in Christ,
in all areas of life.

Silence

O Lord, you are our hope:
you are the hope of the world.

Let us pray for the world of commerce,
trade and the media;
that Christ's peaceful presence
at the heart of business
may make them channels
for enlightenment and discernment,
and instruments for good
in our society.

Silence

O Lord, you are our hope:
you are the hope of the world.

Let us pray for the malnourished,
those whose land no longer supports them;
that all people may be inspired
to care for one another,
to share the world's resources
in mutual trust,
and be living signs of hope
for us all.

Silence

O Lord, you are our hope:
you are the hope of the world.

Let us pray for ourselves and our families,
that our day to day concerns
may not blind us to God's love,
but rather be infused by it
so that he is central in our lives.

Silence

O Lord, you are our hope:
you are the hope of the world.

In the silence of our hearts
we pray to our heavenly Father
about our own particular concerns.

Silence

Lord, we pray in hope;
hear these prayers
for the sake of Jesus, our Saviour.

Amen.

NEW LIFE IN CHRIST

Christ, the Resurrection and the Life

In the presence of the risen Christ,
let us lift our hearts and pray
to God the giver of all life.

We pray for all who are called
to particular ministries
within the Church;
all ordained ministers,
theological students and teachers,
that as they learn together
they may grow in wisdom and humility
and be increasingly filled
with the life of Christ.

Silence

Lord, stand among us:
and give us new life.

We pray for all areas of bureaucracy
which frustrate and delay
the course of useful action;
for all areas of instability
and political corruption;
that whatever is good may flourish and grow,
so that evil may be overcome
and rendered powerless.

Silence

Lord, stand among us:
and give us new life.

We pray for all who suffer from pain or disease,
and those who tend them;
that they may be comforted.
Silence
Lord, stand among us:
and give us new life.

We pray for all who are engaged
or newly married;
for those coping with family problems,
difficult circumstances or bereavement;
that they may lean on
the loving presence of Christ
who dispels all fear
and brings life and peace.
Silence
Lord, stand among us:
and give us new life.

Trustingly, we pray in silence
to our loving Lord
who considers each one of us special.
Silence
Father,
we thank you for your constant
life-renewing love,
and offer these prayers
for the sake of your Son, Jesus Christ.
Amen.

God, the giver of life

Let us bring our lives and concerns
to the Father, from whom all life comes,
trusting in his power and love.

We bring to his love all those
who have committed their lives to Christ
in ordained ministries;
that they may grow into spiritual maturity,
and live always
as freed sons and daughters of God.
Silence
O Lord, you have set us free:
that we may truly live.

We bring to his love the world
and its problems, mistakes
and errors of judgement;
that in every society
the Lord's light may shine
and his life and peace be known.
Silence
O Lord, you have set us free:
that we may truly live.

We bring to his love the deaf,
the blind and the partially sighted,
all those who are chronically ill
and all who tend them;
that even in all their hardships

they may know life in all its fullness.
Silence
O Lord, you have set us free:
that we may truly live.

We bring to his love our own parents,
all adoptive and foster parents,
women labouring to bring new life
into the world,
that they may be blessed and strengthened
by him who is life itself.
Silence
O Lord, you have set us free:
that we may truly live.

Meeting our heavenly Father
in the stillness of silence,
let us express to him
our particular burdens of prayer.
Silence
Father,
we bring these prayers
through Jesus Christ,
through whom we have
life in abundance.
Amen.

Word of eternal life

As followers of Christ,
let us pray together in his presence
to our merciful Father
who feels with us in our needs.

We bring to his love
all religious communities
and organisations
who offer a constant wave of prayer
as the earth spins;
all who sense that God
might be calling them
to a life of renewal
and deeper commitment,
that his will may be made clear to them.
Silence

Lord of all our lives:
hear us, we pray.

We bring to his love
all who wield power
in each community of our world;
those who persist in challenging
injustice and prejudice;
all who bring to public attention
areas of need and unnoticed hardship
where life is stifled or denied.
Silence

Lord of all our lives:
hear us, we pray.

We bring to his love
all those in hospital,
in wards and on operating tables
throughout the world;
those worn down by constant pain;
those who are struggling
to rebuild broken lives.
Silence
Lord of all our lives:
hear us, we pray.

We bring to his love
our own particular concerns,
hopes, doubts and fears;
our difficulties at work and at home,
our responsibilities.
Silence
Lord of all our lives:
hear us, we pray.

In silence,
we name any we know
who especially need our prayer.
Silence
**In great thankfulness
for the gift of life
and for all your blessings to us,
heavenly Father,
we offer you these prayers
through Jesus Christ.**
Amen.

Celebrate resurrection

In the hope and joy of resurrection,
let us pray to the God
who loves us so completely.

We pray for all who have been called by Christ
to serve the world as his followers;
that initial enthusiasm
may not die but deepen
to set us all on fire
with his love.
Silence

Lord of life:
transform us all.

We pray for a fairer distribution
of the world's resources,
so that life and hope
are brought to the starving
and homeless;
for places where fear and violence rule;
that peace and justice may be restored.
Silence

Lord of life:
transform us all.

We pray for those who feel they are wasting
  their lives;
for those under pressure
at home or at work;

for all who feel lost,
uncertain or worthless;
that God's living power
may stabilise, heal and recreate them.
Silence
Lord of life:
transform us all.

We pray for ourselves,
our friends and relatives,
and any difficulties or problems
that may be known to us,
that in all our troubles
we may open ourselves
to the healing and renewing
life of Christ,
which has power to bring hope.
Silence
Lord of life:
transform us all.

In the silence of God's accepting love,
we pray our individual prayers.
Silence
In silence we praise you, Father,
for your abundant blessings,
and ask you to hear these prayers,
for the sake of Jesus Christ.
Amen.

Openness and humility

Let us pray to God our Father,
with humility and love,
open to his transforming grace.

We pray for all Christians
striving to follow the Lord of Life;
that they may not fall
into the temptation of complacency
or self-righteousness;
that they may joyfully become
the least important
for Christ's sake.
Silence
God, our Father:
be merciful to us sinners.

We pray for all who are involved
in the worldly struggles for power,
all areas of political unrest,
all decision and policy-makers;
that wisdom, common sense and respect
may encourage just and peaceful government.
Silence
God, our Father:
be merciful to us sinners.

We pray for the physically blind
and their families;
for those who are spiritually blind

and think they can see;
for those whose minds are confused
through accidents, illness or age,
that God's inner sight
may bring enlightenment, order and peace.
Silence

God, our Father:
be merciful to us sinners.

We pray for ourselves and all those
worshipping in this place,
that we may be increasingly open
to the searing light of Christ,
until our darkest corners are lit by his love.
Silence

God, our Father:
be merciful to us sinners.

In silence, now,
we bring our private concerns to God,
who always hears our prayers of faith.
Silence

Lord God,
accept these prayers,
through Christ our Lord.
Amen.

Good stewardship

We have pledged to commit our lives to Christ;
let us pray, then,
in his Spirit.

We pray that all Christians may witness
to the value of caring,
regardless of race or colour;
that they may be maintained
in the strength and humility of Christ
to serve the world in love.
Silence
Lord, take us:
help us to live.

We pray for all monarchs, presidents,
and those in powerful positions;
for those whom they govern,
and for those with whom they negotiate;
that their great resources of power and wealth
may be so used
that peace and justice may prevail
over all our earth.
Silence
Lord, take us:
help us to live.

We pray for the very poor,
the weak and oppressed,
the abandoned, rejected and abused;

that all obstacles to their healing and wholeness
may be removed,
all blindness, prejudice and greed
transformed through Christ
into an outpouring of love and hope.
Silence

Lord, take us:
help us to live.

We pray for ourselves;
that we may see our own faults more clearly,
acknowledge our weaknesses
as well as our strengths,
and offer both to Christ
who can make us new.
Silence

Lord, take us:
help us to live.

In silence, now,
we pour out to God our Father
any needs and burdens known to us personally.
Silence

Lord God of all creation,
accept these prayers,
though Jesus Christ our Lord.
Amen.

God's Spirit in us

As members of the body of Christ,
let us pray together.

We pray for all those who form the Church,
in its variety and richness
throughout the world;
that we may be encouraged
and strengthened
and our weariness
constantly refreshed
by the living Spirit of Jesus.
Silence

Come to us as we are:
and renew us by your presence.

We pray for all councils, committees
and governing bodies,
for those serving on juries,
for air, sea and mountain rescue teams,
that in working together
and enabled by God's Spirit
they may strive for what is good,
just and honest.
Silence

Come to us as we are:
and renew us by your presence.

We pray for the poor and for the hungry,
for the blind, the downtrodden
and those imprisoned;
that God's Spirit,
alive in his people,
will work his healing love.

Silence

Come to us as we are:
and renew us by your presence.

We pray for ourselves,
that we may be given deeper insight,
more awareness and greater love,
so that we can more effectively
serve the world
as living members
of the body of Christ.

Silence

Come to us as we are:
and renew us by your presence.

We bring our own personal prayers
in silence, now,
to God our loving Father.

Silence

Father,
we ask you to hear our prayers,
through Jesus Christ our Lord.

Amen.

The life of the Spirit

In wonder let us pray
to the almighty and everlasting God.

We pray for the Church,
that in constant prayerfulness
Christians may be attentive
and receptive
to the Holy Spirit.
Silence
Father almighty:
may your Spirit fill us with life.

We pray for the world,
with all its mistakes and tragedies,
that God's active Spirit
will bring order,
serenity and hope.
Silence
Father almighty:
may your Spirit fill us with life.

We pray for those whose lives
are darkened by guilt,
resentment and despair;
for those who live violent and cruel lives;
for drug dealers
and all who corrupt young minds;
that God's generous Spirit of love
will bring light to their hearts.

Silence
Father almighty:
may your Spirit fill us with life.

We pray for our loved ones
and for anyone we find difficult to love;
that God's Spirit living in us
will increase our love
for each other.
Silence
Father almighty:
may your Spirit fill us with life.

Alive to the Holy Spirit,
we name those we know
who are in any particular need.
Silence
Father,
accept these prayers,
through Jesus Christ our Lord.
Amen.

Love one another

As members of the risen body of Christ,
and united in his love,
let us pray
to our heavenly Father.

We pray for the work of the Church
in spreading the Good News of Jesus
who has brought life and hope
to the world.
Silence
Lord God of love:
renew our lives.

We pray for all those with authority
and responsibility
in governing the nations
of this world:
for peace, for compassion,
forgiveness and generosity.
Silence
Lord God of love:
renew our lives.

We pray for those who shut love out;
those who have been hurt
by lack of love;
those whose love
has become distorted
and twisted into hate.

Silence

Lord God of love:
renew our lives.

We pray for those who live and worship here;
for particular areas in our own lives
where the love of God is desperately needed
to transfigure, refresh
and enrich.

Silence

Lord God of love:
renew our lives.

In silence,
we make our private petitions to God,
who knows all our needs.

Silence

Father,
confident in your boundless love,
we place these prayers before you,
through Jesus Christ our Lord.
Amen.

He who was dead is alive

As brothers and sisters in Christ,
let us pray that his risen life
will infuse and activate
all areas of creation.

We pray for the Church,
especially for missionaries
both abroad and in this country;
that with inner quietness
they may be ready to listen
to the voice of the Spirit.
Silence
Father of our risen Lord:
may your Spirit guide us.

We pray for world leaders and their advisers,
that nothing may tempt them from integrity,
and that they may boldly work
for what is good, honest and just.
Silence
Father of our risen Lord:
may your Spirit guide us.

We pray for those who doubt,
those who have lost their faith,
and those whose faith is being tested;
that they may know the assurance
of God's presence and his love.

Silence

Father of our risen Lord:
may your Spirit guide us.

We pray for our own community,
that we may serve Christ
in caring for one another
and encourage one another
in the faith of our loving Lord.

Silence

Father of our risen Lord:
may your Spirit guide us.

In the name of the risen Lord,
we name our own particular cares
and concerns.

Silence

Father,
we know that you are here present;
hear the prayers we make,
confident of your love,
through Jesus Christ our Lord.
Amen.

Christ is risen!

Let us pray
that our world may be transformed
by the light of Christ's resurrection.

We pray that the joy and conviction of Christians
may be so radiant
that all who are lost,
weary and searching
may be directed towards the lasting
inner peace of God.

Silence

Risen Lord:
live in us all.

We pray that from every world crisis and tragedy
some good may come;
that every problem may become an opportunity
for development and spiritual growth.

Silence

Risen Lord:
live in us all.

We pray that those in mental, physical
or spiritual distress
may recognise in their suffering
the seeds from which hope may spring,
looking toward the day when they share
the joy and wholeness of all creation.

Silence
Risen Lord:
live in us all.

We pray for the newly born
and for all families;
that the children may be nurtured,
and the elderly cherished,
in God's wide accepting love.
Silence
Risen Lord:
live in us all.

In and through the power
of the risen Lord,
we bring our private prayers
and thanksgivings.
Silence
Father,
in grateful thanks,
we pray we may be worthy
of all your gifts and blessings.
Hear our prayer
through Christ our risen Lord.
Amen.

The hope of glory

As brothers and sisters
in the risen Christ,
let us pray together
to our loving, merciful Father.

We pray that the Church
may be guided
and strengthened in hope,
and that all Christians
may be attentive to their calling.
Silence
Give us new life:
and use us to your glory.

We pray that all nations
may be led to understand
God's way of love,
and that all decisions
may reflect his will.
Silence
Give us new life:
and use us to your glory.

We pray that the lonely and frightened
may experience the joy of God's peace;
and the despairing may see
in the resurrection
the light of hope.

Silence
Give us new life:
and use us to your glory.

We pray that in all our relationships
we may proclaim the Good News
of God's saving love
by the way we respond to one another.
Silence
Give us new life:
and use us to your glory.

In the silence
which God our Father fills
with love and hope,
we offer our own particular prayers.
Silence
Father,
in deepest joy for the love
you have shown us
we ask you to accept our prayer,
through Jesus Christ our Lord.
Amen.

Joy in commitment

Let us pray together
to our heavenly Father
who, through Jesus Christ,
has adopted us
as his own children.

We pray that the Spirit of God
who anointed Jesus
will strengthen and uphold us
so that we live Christian lives,
flooding the world
with God's saving love.
Silence

Loving Father:
may your will be done.

We pray that all leaders
and those in positions of power
may understand the fundamental need
for God's spirit of truth,
peace and compassion
and commit themselves
to his way of justice.
Silence

Loving Father:
may your will be done.

We pray that any who are living under
a burden of guilt
may be led to complete repentance
and find freedom and joy
in God's forgiveness.
Silence
Loving Father:
may your will be done.

We pray that, being filled
with the life of Christ,
the quality and brightness
of our lives
may draw others into his love
and peace.
Silence
Loving Father:
may your will be done.

In the silence of God's attentive love,
we name those we know
who are in any particular need.
Silence
Father,
confident in your love,
we ask these things,
in Jesus' name.
Amen.

The authority of Christ

Summoned by Christ
to live his risen life,
let us pray
in the assurance of faith
to our heavenly Father.

We pray that many may be receptive
to God's calling
and, acknowledging his authority,
be prepared to relinquish
personal ambitions and plans
in submitting their lives
to his service.
Silence
Lord of creation:
may your will be done.

We pray that the leaders of the nations
may be sensitive to the needs
of their people,
just and merciful,
caring and constructive.
Silence
Lord of creation:
may your will be done.

We pray that all who work to heal,
restore movement, hearing,
sight or speech,

may be blessed as they work
in harmony with God;
that those they tend
may be given courage,
patience and wholeness.

Silence

Lord of creation:
may your will be done.

We pray that in every person we meet this week
we may look for the good
and be alert to needs;
that we may be ready to serve cheerfully,
without grudging,
happy to be serving Christ.

Silence

Lord of creation:
may your will be done.

Now, in the space of silence,
we bring to God our Father
our own private prayers.

Silence

Most merciful Father,
we ask you to accept these prayers,
through Jesus Christ.

Amen.

Responding to God's call

Bound together in the life of Christ,
let us pour out our needs and concerns
before our Lord and Father,
who knows and loves us so well.

We commend to his love
all who have been recently ordained;
that the people to whom they minister
may accept and love them
and help them to grow in Christ.
Silence

Lord, we are here:
we come to do your will.

We commend to his wisdom
all who wield power;
that, recognising God's call
to justice and compassion,
they may encourage reconciliation
rather than revenge,
friendship rather than aggression,
and flexibility,
rather than stubborn intransigence.
Silence

Lord, we are here:
we come to do your will.

We commend to his healing
all who are ill or in pain,

all who are recovering from surgery,
all who depend on others
for life and movement;
any who long for friends
who would visit them in their illness.

Silence

Lord, we are here:
we come to do your will.

We commend to his peace and joy
our homes and all the homes
in this community,
especially any where there is conflict
or distress;
that, being dwelt in by Christ,
our homes may speak to every visitor
of his love.

Silence

Lord, we are here:
we come to do your will.

In silence filled with love,
we name our particular prayer burdens.

Silence

Loving Father,
we thank you for calling us,
and ask you to hear these prayers we offer
through Jesus Christ, our Saviour.
Amen.

Come, Holy Spirit

As the Body of Christ, filled with his Spirit
and bound together in love,
let us pray
for our fellow members in the Church
and for our world.

We pray that all who profess to be Christians
may allow the Spirit
to penetrate their lives,
prune them where necessary,
realign, train and support them
so that they produce good fruit.
Silence
Holy Spirit, hear us:
we open ourselves to you.

We pray that the Holy Spirit may work
through the common bond of humanity
to draw people closer,
develop international understanding
and friendship,
break down prejudice
and generate peace.
Silence
Holy Spirit, hear us:
we open ourselves to you.

We pray that all who are damaged
and scarred physically,

mentally, emotionally or spiritually
may be given wholeness and healing;
and that all who are floundering and confused
may find assurance in Christ,
the source of meaning,
through his indwelling Spirit.

Silence

Holy Spirit, hear us:
we open ourselves to you.

We pray that we may use
the gifts of the Spirit within us to the full,
walking cheerfully and thankfully
in the way God has prepared for us,
and delighting in every opportunity to serve.

Silence

Holy Spirit, hear us:
we open ourselves to you.

Refreshed in the Holy Spirit,
we approach our loving Father
with our private petitions.

Silence

Loving Father,
rejoicing in your strength
and fellowship,
we lay these prayers before you,
through Jesus Christ our Lord.
Amen.

Christ makes us whole

As sharers in Christ's risen life,
in trust and thankfulness
let us pray to the Lord.

We pray for the work of the Church
in every country,
especially where Christian witness
brings danger;
that the Spirit of Christ
may nurture life and hope
in the world's darkest areas.
Silence

Risen Lord:
instil in us your peace.

We pray for all who encourage others
to squander their time,
money or talents;
all who lead others into drug addiction;
that they may come to know Christ
as the only treasure worth worshipping.
Silence

Risen Lord:
instil in us your peace.

We pray for all whose characters
have become hardened and twisted
through jealousy, resentment or hatred;
that they may at last recognise

their need for repentance
and come to Christ to be restored
to the joy of new life in him.
Silence
Risen Lord:
instil in us your peace.

We pray for those who helped
to bring us to know Christ,
and those who turn us back to him
when we wander away;
that in humility we may always be glad to learn
and ready to accept criticism,
in order to grow as Christians.
Silence
Risen Lord:
instil in us your peace.

We name in silence now
any known to us
with particular needs and burdens.
Silence
Heavenly Father,
slow to anger and quick to forgive;
immerse us in your Spirit
and let your will be done in our lives,
through Jesus Christ our Lord.
Amen.

Christ shows God's glory

Bound together in love
by the power of the Holy Spirit,
let us pray
to our heavenly Father.

We pray for all newly baptised Christians,
all preparing for baptism,
and everyone involved
in teaching the faith;
that Christ's love may take root,
grow, and produce good fruit
to the glory of God.
Silence

Father of Jesus:
use us for your glory

We pray for the world's political leaders
and all who influence them;
that there may be mutual respect and courtesy,
and a shared desire
for peace and understanding.
Silence

Father of Jesus:
use us for your glory

We pray for those who carry heavy burdens
of guilt or anxiety;
for the very ill and the dying
and for their loved ones

who share their suffering;
that the Spirit of Christ will comfort,
soothe and strengthen them.

Silence

Father of Jesus:
use us for your glory

We pray for ourselves
and our spiritual development;
for all whom we irritate and annoy;
for any we have unwittingly hurt or damaged;
that in fixing our gaze on Jesus,
we may see our true selves more clearly.

Silence

Father of Jesus:
use us for your glory

Conscious of the Holy Spirit among us,
we share with God our Father
our personal burdens, joys and sorrows.

Silence

Father, we rejoice
in your uncompromising love for us,
and ask you to hear our prayers,
through Jesus Christ our Lord.

Amen.

Repent: the kingdom is near

As children of our caring
heavenly Father,
let us pray for the coming
of his kingdom.

We pray for all Christians
throughout the world;
that they may wholeheartedly follow Christ,
so that their lives witness to the beauty
and peace of his kingdom.
Silence
Father of love:
remake our lives.

We pray for all world leaders,
governments and their advisers;
that they may be inspired
to lead their people wisely and fairly,
with understanding and sensitivity.
Silence
Father of love:
remake our lives.

We pray for all those who feel trapped
by the emotional, financial
or political circumstances
of their lives;

that in Christ they may find
freedom and vitality.
Silence
Father of love:
remake our lives.

We pray for our own families and loved ones,
especially any from whom we are separated;
that we may learn to see Christ in each face,
and serve him in caring for each other.
Silence
Father of love:
remake our lives.

Together in silence
we make our private prayers
and thanksgivings.
Silence
Father of all time and space,
accept these prayers
through Jesus Christ our Lord.
Amen.

FAITH, TRUST, HOPE

Hope in Christ

Let us pray in hope
to our heavenly Father,
trusting in his infinite mercy.

We pray for all Christian people,
especially those whose faith
has been battered
through disaster and suffering;
that they may know
the assurance of God's abiding presence
which transforms and rebuilds.
Silence
Touch our lives, Lord:
that we may live in hope.

We pray for all administrative bodies
and political institutions;
that they may be always aware
of the real needs of those they serve,
and be effective
in providing for them.
Silence
Touch our lives, Lord:
that we may live in hope.

We pray for the dying
and those who love and tend them;
for the bereaved and desolate;
that they may draw strength

from the reality of Christ's life
and his victory over death.
Silence
Touch our lives, Lord:
that we may live in hope.

We pray for our local community
with all its needs and cares;
that we may be ready to serve Christ
in our area
and spread his life-giving hope and joy.
Silence
Touch our lives, Lord:
that we may live in hope.

We know that our Father is listening;
in silence we bring to him
our own particular needs or concerns.
Silence
God our Father,
hear our prayer
and help us to do your will,
through Jesus Christ our Lord.

Faithfulness

In faith,
knowing that where two or three
are gathered in Jesus' name,
he will grant their requests,
let us pray.

We pray for the Church,
that all Christian leaders
may be given insight and understanding
to guide their people
into the light of God's truth.
Silence

Lord, we believe:
help our unbelief.

We pray for all councils, committees
and conferences,
that a spirit of integrity
may underlie all discussion
and a desire for goodness
inspire all decisions.
Silence

Lord, we believe:
help our unbelief.

We pray for those in pain or distress,
physically, emotionally
or spiritually;
that they may hold to God

through all the bad times,
trusting in his love
which never fails.
Silence
Lord, we believe:
help our unbelief.

We pray for all families,
especially those who have troubles;
that they may not be damaged
through their suffering,
but rather grow
in compassion and understanding.
Silence
Lord, we believe:
help our unbelief.

Knowing that God our Father
hears the prayers of his children,
we pray in silence
our own individual prayers.
Silence
Father,
we ask all this
through Jesus Christ our Lord.
Amen.

God awaits our response

God our Father loves us
and longs for us to respond.
Coming together in faith,
let us pray to him now
for the Church
and for the world.

We pray for a deeper trustfulness
among all Christian people,
so that they may become
more and more open
to God's will.
Silence

Lord, our Redeemer:
deepen our love.

We pray that Love may make his home
in the hearts of people
all over the world,
to guide, sustain
and renew.
Silence

Lord, our Redeemer:
deepen our love.

We pray that every family
may become filled
with the life of Christ
and know his joy

and his transforming love.

Silence

Lord, our Redeemer:
deepen our love.

We pray for all expectant mothers,
for the children growing within them,
for the babies being born today,
and for those children
who are neglected or abused.

Silence

Lord, our Redeemer:
deepen our love.

We pray to our loving Father
in silence,
for everything we need.

Silence

In thankfulness we ask you, Father,
to hear our prayers,
through Christ our Lord.

Amen.

Loving and trusting God

As we share a common faith and hope,
let us pray trustingly together
to the God who made us
and sustains us.

Let us pray for all
who profess themselves Christians;
that in fastening our eyes on Christ
we may be led to unity.
Silence
Father almighty:
our life is in your hands.

Let us pray for the political, industrial
and commercial administrations
throughout our planet;
that our material and economic organisation
may reveal good stewardship
of the gifts God has provided.
Silence
Father almighty:
our life is in your hands.

Let us pray for all convicted prisoners,
and for the victims of their crimes;
for all who are eaten up
with hatred or jealousy;
for all who are finding it impossible
to forgive their enemies.

Silence
Father almighty:
our life is in your hands.

Let us pray for the homes and families
represented here;
for our loved ones
from whom we are separated
by distance or death;
for a deepening love towards each other
in all our relationships.
Silence

Father almighty:
our life is in your hands.

In the silence of our hearts,
we pray for any needs
known to us personally.
Silence

Father,
with grateful thanks for the gift of life,
we offer you these prayers
together with ourselves
for your service;
in Jesus' name we pray.
Amen.

Wholeness and harmony

As members of the Church of Christ,
let us lay our needs and cares
at the feet of our heavenly Father.

We ask that his love, peace and joy
may fill the Church
in every corner of the earth;
that God's name may be held holy
in unending waves of praise.
Silence
Unchanging Lord:
fix our hearts on your goodness.

We ask that all negotiators
and administrators
may be guided to work with sensitivity,
care and integrity.
Silence
Unchanging Lord:
fix our hearts on your goodness.

We ask that all strained marriages
may be healed and strengthened;
that those whose lives
have been damaged or warped
may be emotionally repaired
and rebuilt.

Silence
Unchanging Lord:
fix our hearts on your goodness.

We ask that our homes may be built
on the solid rock of Christ,
so that when storms come
they may stand firm.
Silence
Unchanging Lord:
fix our hearts on your goodness.

Knowing that God our Father
hears the cry of his children,
we pray in silence
for our needs and cares.
Silence
Father of compassion and mercy,
accept our prayers,
through the person of Jesus Christ.
Amen.

Struggling with faith

As brothers and sisters in Christ,
let us pray
with confidence and faith
to the true and living God.

We pray for the newly baptised
and the recently ordained;
for those who have rejected
their former faith,
and those who are besieged by doubt.
Silence
Father of heaven:
protect and bless them all.

We pray for those under pressure,
who are tempted
to compromise God's values
of truth and love;
for all who make
far-reaching decisions.
Silence
Father of heaven:
protect and bless them all.

We pray for all the victims of power struggles,
suffering poverty, neglect,
disease and malnutrition;
for all whose health has been wrecked
by insanitary living and working conditions.

Silence
Father of heaven:
protect and bless them all.

We pray for ourselves,
for our neighbours and our friends,
for any we have hurt or offended;
for any who have hurt or offended us.
Silence
Father of heaven:
protect and bless them all.

Together in silence now,
we offer our own private prayers.
Silence
Most loving and merciful Father,
we ask you to take over our lives
and live through them,
and accept these our prayers
in the name of Jesus.
Amen.

Let the seeds grow

Rooted in Christ,
let us call to mind now
all those in need, and pray for them
to our heavenly Father.

We pray that all who teach the Christian faith
may be given appropriate language
to get through to those who hear,
so that the word of God takes root
in many hearts.
Silence
Lord of life:
help us to grow.

We pray that all diplomats and negotiators
may promote peace and friendship
between the nations,
fostering mutual respect
and understanding.
Silence
Lord of life:
help us to grow.

We pray that those whose lifestyle
has been threatened or shattered
by crippling illness or injury
may find within their suffering
the seeds of hope,
bringing new meaning to their lives

and transforming their outlook.
Silence
Lord of life:
help us to grow.

We pray that we and our families,
neighbours and friends
may become daily more Christlike
and less self-centred;
more responsive to the needs of those around us,
and less bothered by what we as individuals
get out of life.
Silence
Lord of life:
help us to grow.

Knowing that God our Father is listening,
we pray in silence
for our own needs and cares.
Silence
Father,
we lay our needs and cares before you,
and ask you to hear us,
through Jesus Christ our Lord.
Amen.

Trust in Jesus

In the Sprit of Jesus,
let us pray to our heavenly Father.

We bring to his love
all those who are being trained
for ministry in the Church;
that their studies may teach them
not only knowledge but perception,
not only skills but sensitivity.
Silence
Guide us, heavenly Father:
to trust in your Son.

We bring to his love
all whose positions of responsibility
cause pressure and stress;
that in their weakness and weariness
they may come to Christ for refreshment,
and rely upon him for their strength.
Silence
Guide us, heavenly Father:
to trust in your Son.

We bring to his love all who are dying;
that their trust in Jesus may deepen,
until their fears are calmed
and they can look forward with real hope
to meeting their Saviour face to face.

Silence

Guide us, heavenly Father:
to trust in your Son.

We bring to his love
our own friends and loved ones;
all who live with us and near us;
all who rely on us,
and all who are influenced
by our behaviour.

Silence

Guide us, heavenly Father:
to trust in your Son.

In silence, now,
we bring to our heavenly Father
our own particular concerns.

Silence

God of all mercy,
our hope and our joy,
we ask you to hear our prayers,
through Jesus Christ our Lord.
Amen.

Out of death, life

Filled with the hope and joy
of resurrection faith,
let us pray confidently
to our loving Father.

We pray for the newly baptised
and their families;
for those who are sensing God's call
and need reassurance in it;
for all God's people
in every part of the world.
Silence
Life-giving Lord:
reign in our hearts.

We pray for the areas in which there is fighting,
unrest and unresolved conflict;
for the unprincipled, the corrupt
and those who thirst for revenge.
Silence
Life-giving Lord:
reign in our hearts.

We pray for those who are finding life difficult
at the moment;
for those who are coping
with personal tragedy or mourning;
for all who are ill or frail.

Silence

Life-giving Lord:
reign in our hearts.

We pray for neighbours here; in our street;
and at school and at work;
for any who may be wishing
they knew someone
willing to share their burden.

Silence

Life-giving Lord:
reign in our hearts.

We pray for our own intentions now,
in silence filled with joy.

Silence

Father,
in the name of the risen Jesus,
we ask you to bring the hope,
healing and joy of the resurrection
to all these people for whom we pray.

Amen.

Love beyond price

Trusting in the deep love
our heavenly Father has for us,
let us pray.

We pray for the grace and strength
to be obedient, as Christ was,
in whatever God asks us to do,
without thought
for our personal gain or safety.
Silence
Wise and loving Father:
may your will be done.

We pray for greater trust and friendship
between the different nations
on our planet;
for a universal desire for peace,
and the willingness to take
the risks it demands.
Silence
Wise and loving Father:
may your will be done.

We pray for Christ's calming reassurance
to bring peace of mind and spirit
to those worried about the future,
those dreading some difficult event,
and those who are frightened of dying.

Silence

Wise and loving Father:
may your will be done.

We pray for the capacity to be positive
and encouraging
in all our relationships;
for the right words to say
in order to be peacemakers
and witnesses to God's
immeasurable love.

Silence

Wise and loving Father:
may your will be done.

We pray to our heavenly Father,
in silence,
about our own particular concerns.

Silence

Father,
with thankful hearts
we offer these concerns
for the Church and for the world,
though Jesus Christ, our Saviour.

Amen.

The risk of faith

As children of God,
let us confide
in our heavenly Father,
who knows us so well.

Into this enlightenment
and perception
we bring all whose faith is limited
by fear or prejudice;
all whose living faith
has been replaced
by the empty shell of habit.
Silence

Lord, we believe:
please help our faith to grow.

Into the depths of his wisdom
and understanding
we bring those with responsibilities,
and all who have difficult decisions to make;
all those in charge of hospitals,
schools, factories
and all community services.
Silence

Lord, we believe:
please help our faith to grow.

Into the gentleness of his healing love
we bring all who are in pain;
all those recovering from surgery;
those involved in crippling accidents
or suffering from wasting diseases.
Silence
Lord, we believe:
please help our faith to grow.

Into his tireless faithfulness
we bring any who rely on us
for help, support,
guidance or encouragement;
any whom we are being asked to serve
or introduce to God's love.
Silence
Lord, we believe:
please help our faith to grow.

We pray in silence, now,
for our individual needs and concerns.
Silence
Father,
whose character is always full of mercy,
hear our prayers
through the pleading of your Son,
Jesus Christ.
Amen.

Let faith be real

As brothers and sisters in Christ,
and children of God our heavenly Father,
let us draw near and tell him
of our needs and cares,
asking for his help and blessing.

Let us ask God to bless and encourage
all those who serve him;
to inspire their teaching,
nudge their memories,
instruct them through their failure
and mature them through their experiences,
so that in all their undertakings,
God's will may be done.
Silence
Merciful Father:
work on us until we shine with love.

Let us ask God to direct and guide
the people of the world
towards harmony and peace,
mutual respect and appreciation
of one another's cultures and traditions;
so that we are prepared to learn from each other.
Silence
Merciful Father:
work on us until we shine with love.

Let us ask God to ease the burdens
of those who are bowed down
with grief, depression,
pain or guilt;
to encourage the timid and frightened;
refresh all who are overworked
or have been unable to sleep,
and break down all barricades
of hatred and revenge.

Silence

Merciful Father:
work on us until we shine with love.

Let us ask God into our homes
and places of work;
so that all friendships
and business transactions,
shopping and leisure time
may be opportunities for rejoicing in his love
and spreading his peace.

Silence

Merciful Father:
work on us until we shine with love.

We name our particular prayer burdens now,
in silence filled with love.

Silence

Father,
in your love accept our prayers,
in Jesus' name.

Amen.

God saves and sends us

Let us pray trustingly
to our heavenly Father
who cares for us.

We pray for those involved in missionary work
all over the world;
that their work may be blessed and fruitful,
and that they may be constantly
strengthened and encouraged
by the caring presence of Christ.
Silence
Call us, loving God:
and send us out in your name.

We pray for the leaders and advisers
of all nations;
for diplomats, envoys and negotiators
in all areas of difficulty,
where tact and delicacy are needed;
that people may learn to respect
and honour one another.
Silence
Call us, loving God:
and send us out in your name.

We pray for all who are harassed and dejected,
overworked, stressed or bewildered;
that they may come to know
the liberating calm of God's peace

beneath all the activity and clamour.
Silence
Call us, loving God:
and send us out in your name.

We pray for increased trust and faithfulness
in our own lives;
for clearer knowledge of God's will
in how our time and ability is used;
for a greater readiness
to listen to God's voice
and respond to his calling.
Silence
Call us, loving God:
and send us out in your name.

In a time of silence
we share with God our Father
our personal burdens, joys and sorrows.
Silence
Father,
we ask you to hear these prayers
through Jesus Christ
our Saviour and brother.
Amen.

The assurance of things not seen

As brothers and sisters in Christ,
with our fellowship rooted
in the love God has for us all,
let us pray to him now.

We pray for the deepening of faith
among all Christians;
that our whole lives may rest
in the joy and security of knowing
that our God is alive and in charge.
Silence
Christ is alive for ever:
our God reigns!

We pray for the spreading of the Good News
throughout the world,
so that whatever important decisions are made
and policies planned,
people may work,
in harmony with their creator,
for goodness, peace and reconciliation.
Silence
Christ is alive for ever:
our God reigns!

We pray for the healing
and repairing of broken lives,

for vision and enlightenment
among those darkened by fear and hatred;
that God's living Spirit, let loose,
may anoint and soothe,
pacify and recharge.

Silence

Christ is alive for ever:
our God reigns!

We pray for a more loving atmosphere
in our homes, our church and community;
more care and concern for each other,
more willingness to forgive,
understand and respect
those with whom we live.

Silence

Christ is alive for ever:
our God reigns!

Knowing that God loves us
personally and with full understanding,
we offer our private prayers
to him in silence.

Silence

Father,
coming together with thanks and praise
to worship you,
we ask you to accept these prayers,
for the sake of Jesus Christ.
Amen.

God confronts the world in Christ

Knowing that our Father loves us,
let us come to him,
as brothers and sisters in Christ,
with our prayers.

Let us pray for more courage
among all Christians;
that they may stand up
against evil and injustice,
wherever they find it,
trusting in God's power
and without thought for personal safety.
Silence
Lord, speak in our hearts:
and we will listen.

Let us pray for those countries at war;
those between whom
there is distrust and suspicion;
that peace may never be dismissed
as impossible,
but acknowledged
as the only real victory.
Silence
Lord, speak in our hearts:
and we will listen.

Let us pray for those who are living
through a personal crisis at the moment;
those who do not know which way
to turn for the best;
that God's will may be made clear to them,
so that they are guided and comforted.

Silence

Lord, speak in our hearts:
and we will listen.

Let us pray for our own lives,
and those of our families,
that we may all know what work
God is calling us to do,
and trust him enough to obey his will.

Silence

Lord, speak in our hearts:
and we will listen.

We pray in silence
for those known to us
who have particular needs.

Silence

Father,
your glory fills and confronts the world,
and so we entrust our cares to you.
in the name of Jesus.
Amen.

Christ has overcome evil

As followers of the way of Christ,
let us bring to the Lord
the needs of our times.

We pray for God's blessing
on all who confess belief in him;
that they may witness powerfully
to his unselfish love and humility
by the way they act
and the lives they lead.
Silence
Father, lead us:
free us from all that is evil.

We pray for God's blessing
on all who administer justice,
those working in law courts,
all who are serving on juries,
and those who make laws,
that they may be given insight
and integrity.
Silence
Father, lead us:
free us from all that is evil.

We pray for God's blessing
on all those in prison or on probation;
all those living in acute poverty;
on all who are working among them

to heal, redirect, support and encourage.

Silence

Father, lead us:
free us from all that is evil.

We pray for God's blessing on us
as we examine our lives
and draw closer to him;
that through our self-discipline and prayer
we may enter God's stillness,
and know his will for us.

Silence

Father, lead us:
free us from all that is evil.

In silence, now,
we approach our loving Father
with our private prayers.

Silence

Father,
accept these prayers,
through Jesus Christ our Lord.

Amen.

Grace and strength come from God

As brothers and sisters in Christ,
let us bring our needs and cares
to the mercy of our heavenly Father.

Let us pray for deepening of prayerfulness
among all Christians,
that firmer faith and greater openness
will lead to a rediscovery
of the love and the purpose of God.
Silence

Father of mercy:
we turn to you for help.

Let us pray for our world,
especially for areas of degradation
and moral decay;
that there may be a turning away
from self-indulgence to self-discipline;
from deception to integrity;
from lawlessness to ordered peace.
Silence

Father of mercy:
we turn to you for help.

Let us pray for those
who have been damaged or injured
through violent abuse, or terrorism;

for all victims of war and rebellion,
and for those who are responsible.

Silence

Father of mercy:
we turn to you for help.

Let us pray for God's strength
in our own lives,
especially in those areas
we know to be weak and open to temptation;
that we may rely more and more on his power
so that we live in him and he in us.

Silence

Father of mercy:
we turn to you for help.

The God of peace is listening:
in this silence
we name our particular concerns.

Silence

Father, hear the prayers of your people,
for the sake of Jesus Christ.

Amen.

Wholeness and unity

Let us approach our heavenly Father
in humility,
as we bring to his love
our cares.

Let us bring to him
the divided Christian community;
that he may bring about wholeness and unity.
Silence
Jesus! Master!
you alone can make us whole.

Let us bring to him
the divided world,
split between wealth and poverty,
complacency and oppression;
that he may break through barriers
with the power of love
and reconciliation.
Silence
Jesus! Master!
you alone can make us whole.

Let us bring to him
all who are disfigured by disease,
disadvantaged mentally or physically,
and all whom society prefers to ignore;
that his love may nourish and heal,
restore and accept.

Silence

Jesus! Master!
you alone can make us whole.

Let us bring to him
the wounds and hurts of our own lives
and our families;
all unresolved tensions and sorrows,
all reunions, joys and healing;
that he will bless our lives with his presence.

Silence

Jesus! Master!
you alone can make us whole.

Confident in God's welcoming love,
we pray in silence, now,
for any needs known to us personally.

Silence

Heavenly Father,
to whom all glory belongs,
accept our prayers,
through Christ our Lord.

Amen.

Complete forgiveness

Let us pray in humility
to our merciful Father.

We pray for the Church, the body of Christ;
for each one of its members who has lapsed
or drifted away;
for those who are struggling
against doubt and temptation.
Silence
Father, forgive:
and lead us safely home.

We pray for the many peoples of this earth;
for the spread of justice,
respect and goodwill;
for a greater capacity to forgive
and restore,
and a weakening
of hardened revenge.
Silence
Father, forgive:
and lead us safely home.

We pray for those who suffer through neglect,
famine, natural disasters or war;
also for those who,
through their own fault,
now suffer.

Silence
Father, forgive:
and lead us safely home.

We pray for each other;
for those we find difficult
to get on with,
those we envy, admire or despise,
that our love may be open and generous,
wide and strong.
Silence
Father, forgive:
and lead us safely home.

Together in silence,
we name those known to us
who especially need our prayer.
Silence
Merciful Father,
accept these prayers,
in the name of our Saviour Jesus Christ.
Amen.

Welcoming Christ

In stillness let us pray
to our heavenly Father.

We lay before him the misunderstandings,
mistakes and foolishness
in the members of Christ's body, the Church;
that through teaching us humility
and forgiveness
even our weaknesses may become
a source of strength and renewal.
Silence
Lord of all:
we welcome you into our lives.

We lay before him all worldly distrust,
revenge and corruption,
all deceit and injustice;
that God's loving Spirit may inspire,
guide, repair and renew,
even where the darkness is deepest.
Silence
Lord of all:
we welcome you into our lives.

We lay before him all those whose busy lives
leave little time for stillness;
the overworked,
those suffering from stress and exhaustion;
that they may find God's inner peace

and constant strength and refreshment.
Silence
Lord of all:
we welcome you into our lives.

We lay before him all the relationships
in our everyday lives;
the ordering of our own timetable;
that living closely with Christ
we may learn how to make room
for the important things
of eternal significance.
Silence
Lord of all:
we welcome you into our lives.

In the silence
of God's attentive love,
we bring our private prayers.
Silence
God our Father,
hear our prayer;
we ask you to help us fix our lives on you,
through Jesus Christ our Lord.
Amen.

Peace

In the peace of our Creator and sustainer,
let us pray.

We pray for the Church throughout the world,
especially in areas of apathy,
and rejection of spiritual values;
that through Christian witness
many may come to find peace
and fulfilment
in Jesus, the Saviour.
Silence
Heavenly Father:
give us your peace.

We pray for all places of conflict;
for countries at war,
for all areas of violence
and bloodshed,
bitterness and hatred.
Silence
Heavenly Father:
give us your peace.

We pray for all who are distressed, bewildered,
lost or confused;
for those making painful decisions;
for those who have no one to turn to for help;
that they may be given guidance,
comfort and serenity.

Silence

Heavenly Father:

give us your peace.

We pray for ourselves,
the special needs and concerns known to us,
for our own spiritual growth;
that our ordered lives may proclaim
the beauty of God's peace.

Silence

Heavenly Father:

give us your peace.

God our Father loves us;
in silence we offer
our personal prayers to him now.

Silence

Father,
knowing that you alone
have the words of eternal life,
we lay our prayers before you.
Through Christ our Lord.

Amen.

Living our faith

Let us pray to God our Father,
bringing before him
our needs and concerns.

We pray for the Church,
its leaders and all the faithful;
that in setting our hearts steadfastly
on the eternal truth of God's love,
we may be nourished
and yield good fruit.
Silence

Lord, support us:
make us whole and strong.

We pray for those working in news coverage
in the media;
for all whose words influence our human society;
that integrity and honour may be valued
and responsibility never abused.
Silence

Lord, support us:
make us whole and strong.

We pray for those who delight
in scandal and gossip,
and for those whose reputations
are damaged by others,
that God's love will heal and renew,
challenge and convert.

Silence

Lord, support us:
make us whole and strong.

We pray for this church fellowship,
its worship, learning and social groups,
that our genuine love for one another,
and desire for one another's good,
may cleanse our hearts from all envy,
intolerance or spitefulness.

Silence

Lord, support us:
make us whole and strong.

In silence, now,
we name any known to us
with particular needs or burdens.

Silence

God our Father,
in our weakness may we rely
on your constant and almighty strength.
We ask you to hear our prayer,
through Jesus Christ our Lord.

Amen.

Trust in God brings peace and joy

Gathered together in faith
before our heavenly Father,
let us bring him
our burdens and cares.

We bring to him
all who teach the Christian faith
by word and example;
that Christ will work,
even through their weakness,
to reach the world.
Silence

Abba, Father:
we belong to you.

We bring to him
all who are striving
for peace and harmony
in local government,
national and international negotiations;
that nothing may deter or divert them,
so that the Father's will
may be done on earth.
Silence

Abba, Father:
we belong to you.

We bring to him all who trust
in worldly solutions or systems,
those whose ideals lead them
not to peace but to violence;
that they may see the great rewards
which come from living and trusting
in a God of selfless love.

Silence

Abba, Father:
we belong to you.

We bring to him our personal faith,
and our lack of faith;
our own efforts to reconcile,
and our sorrow for where these have failed;
we offer him ourselves
and ask him to increase our faith and trust.

Silence

Abba, Father:
we belong to you.

Together now in silence,
we pray our individual prayers
to our heavenly Father.

Silence

We commend all our cares
to the God who loves us as his children,
through Jesus Christ our Lord.

Amen.

Love is the greatest gift

Let us pray
to our heavenly Father,
trusting not in ourselves,
but in his mercy.

We pray for a constant renewal
in the Church;
for a ceaseless deepening of love
and thankfulness.
Silence
Loving Father:
teach us your ways.

We pray for the world in which we live;
for more tolerance
and forgiveness
among its people;
for more understanding
and less fear;
for more friendship
and less bitterness.
Silence
Loving Father:
teach us your ways.

We pray for all who hate,
for all who seek revenge,
for all who refuse to forgive;
that love may transform

their hearts and minds.
Silence
Loving Father:
teach us your ways.

We pray for the people next to us here;
that, being open to the grace of God,
our community may be more deeply filled
with his Spirit of outgoing love.
Silence
Loving Father:
teach us your ways.

In the silence of God's attentive love,
we name those we know
who are in particular need.
Silence
God our Father,
hear these prayers;
give us all those qualities of faith,
hope and love
which last for ever.
In Jesus' name we pray.
Amen.

Christt, the Good Shepherd

As followers of the Good Shepherd,
let us bring with us the needs
of all our brothers and sisters.
Let us pray together.

We pray for the Church,
that in its various ministries
it may never lead any astray,
but always follow faithfully
the way of Jesus Christ
the Good Shepherd.

Silence

Guide us, Father:
along the right path.

We pray for the world,
that in striving to do God's will
we may not abuse or waste our talents
in thoughtless destruction,
but rather work with our Creator
to heal, conserve and fulfil.

Silence

Guide us, Father:
along the right path.

We pray for those who are ill,
and those who look after them;
that even in pain and discomfort
they may recognise Christ,

who also suffered,
and who is full of caring
and compassion.
Silence
Guide us, Father:
along the right path.

We pray for all of us here,
and the families we represent;
that in following Jesus, the Shepherd,
we may be liberated
to live selfless, generous lives.
Silence
Guide us, Father:
along the right path.

In a time of silence
we share with God our Father
our personal burdens, joys and sorrows.
Silence
Father,
hear our prayer;
in joy may we follow the way of Christ,
who alone has the words of eternal life,
through the same Jesus Christ, our Lord.
Amen.

God seeks the lost

While we are still far off
from God our Father,
he comes to welcome us,
and so we pray.

We remember all lapsed Christians,
all who have lost their faith;
that they may return to God
and find him ready
to welcome them home.
Silence
Father of love:
let your kingdom come.

We remember all
who have been made redundant,
all whose work is unhealthy,
or dangerous;
that we may strive to uphold
each person's dignity
and ease each person's burden.
Silence
Father of love:
let your kingdom come.

We remember the rejected and the homeless,
those who have become bitter and twisted
or hard and mean;
that the generous warmth of God's love

will work within them
to thaw what is frozen,
strengthen what is weak,
heal what is hurt
and repair what is damaged.

Silence

Father of love:
let your kingdom come.

We remember our homes,
that they may spread the Good News
of Christ's redeeming love
by the way they reflect his peace,
his understanding and his joy.

Silence

Father of love:
let your kingdom come.

We know that our merciful Father hears us;
let us pray in silence now
for our individual needs.

Silence

Father,
hear our prayers,
through Jesus Christ our Lord.
Amen.

Be reconciled to God

Let us pray for spiritual growth
in the Church and the world.

We pray that the good news of God's salvation
may never be taken for granted
but accepted and shared
with thankfulness and joy.
Silence
Life-giving God:
heal this world.

We pray that all nations may have courage
to fight against what is evil
and to nurture what is good
in an atmosphere of respect
and consideration for others.
Silence
Life-giving God:
heal this world.

We pray for those whose lives
have been twisted and spoilt by sin;
that the lost and weary
may turn to the God of love
for guidance and peace.
Silence
Life-giving God:
heal this world.

We pray for all those living in this district;
that we may use our gifts
in serving one another
and spreading the love of Jesus
throughout the world.

Silence

Life-giving God:
heal this world.

God our Father loves us;
in silence we bring
our personal prayers to him now.

Silence

Father, we ask all these things
through Jesus Christ our Lord.

Amen.

Jesus gives sight to the blind

Bound together in the Spirit of Christ,
let us pray together
to our heavenly Father.

We pray that wherever there is blindness,
prejudice or lack of vision in the Church,
Christ will work his healing power
to refresh, enlighten and transform.
Silence

Not our will, Lord:
but yours be done.

We pray that wherever personality conflicts,
errors of judgement or insensitivity
threaten peace,
God's Spirit may be allowed access,
to work towards harmony and goodwill.
Silence

Not our will, Lord:
but yours be done.

We pray that all who are troubled and distressed
by pain, illness,
poverty, hunger
or any other suffering,
may experience the personal love
and loyalty

of the healing Christ.

Silence

Not our will, Lord:
but yours be done.

We pray that we may be more sensitive
to the needs of those with whom
we live and work,
less critical,
and better prepared
to encourage and forgive.

Silence

Not our will, Lord:
but yours be done.

To God our heavenly Father,
we pray for our own intentions.

Silence

Father,
you pour out your blessings so richly on us;
with thankful hearts we praise you,
and ask you to hear our prayers,
through Jesus Christ our Lord.

Amen.

Overcome evil with good

As trustful children,
let us confide in our loving Father,
and pour out to him
our fears and concerns.

We pray for all lapsed Christians
and all whose faith is being tested;
all whose spiritual growth is being stunted
by material cares or possessions;
and all who are hesitantly approaching Jesus
for the first time
or after long separation from him.
Silence

Almighty Father:
your grace is sufficient for us.

We pray for the areas in which corruption
has splintered the integrity of government;
for the instances
of double dealing and hypocrisy,
which blunt honour
and breed suspicion and revenge.
Silence

Almighty Father:
your grace is sufficient for us.

We pray for all who are trapped and frustrated
by physical or mental disabilities,
illness or weakness;
for the lonely
and those for whom no one prays.
Silence
Almighty Father:
your grace is sufficient for us.

We pray for enlightenment as to our own areas
of spiritual weakness;
for the courage to desire real,
fundamental changes there,
and for the will to persevere in growing.
Silence
Almighty Father:
your grace is sufficient for us.

In silence now,
we approach our loving Father
with our private prayers.
Silence
Most merciful Father,
who knows us so well,
accept our prayers
in the name of Jesus.
Amen.

God has power to forgive

Knowing the deep love that surrounds us
and reaches out to us in every distress,
let us unload our burdens of care
to the healing power
of our heavenly Father

We bring before him the Church's work
among the homeless,
the disillusioned and the apathetic,
in communities
all over the world.
Silence
Life-giving Lord:
hear us and help us, we pray.

We bring before him
all areas of the world
where lack of communication
breeds suspicion and fear;
where lack of understanding
breeds insecurity
and a spirit of revenge.
Silence
Life-giving Lord:
hear us and help us, we pray.

We bring before him all whose lives
are crippled by unrepented sin
or the refusal to forgive;

all whose lives are constantly restless
and devoid of peace.

Silence

Life-giving Lord:
hear us and help us, we pray.

We bring before him
each member of this community,
each anxiety and sorrow,
each hope and dream,
each weakness and special need.

Silence

Life-giving Lord:
hear us and help us, we pray.

Confident in God's restoring love,
we pray silently now
for our personal concerns.

Silence

Heavenly Father,
so full of power
and yet so personally involved with us,
accept these prayers
and let your will be done in our lives,
through Jesus Christ we pray.

Amen.

Return to God

Let us come before God
our Creator and sustainer,
with the needs of the Church
and of the world.

We bring to his love
all who have committed their lives
to his service;
that they may all be one,
bound together
by God's Holy Spirit.
Silence
Father of mercy:
hear us with compassion.

We bring to his love
all the areas of the world
in which there is hostility and unrest;
that new routes to negotiation
and reconciliation may emerge.
Silence
Father of mercy:
hear us with compassion.

We bring to his love
all who have become hard and aggressive
through years of festering hate or jealousy;
that their unresolved conflicts
may be brought to God's light and healed.

Silence

Father of mercy:
hear us with compassion.

We bring to his love
the members of our human families,
especially any we find it difficult
to get on with or understand;
that our love for one another
may enter a new dimension
of warm and positive caring,
seasoned with laughter.

Silence

Father of mercy:
hear us with compassion.

In silence now we offer
our personal prayers to God our Father.

Silence

Lord and Father,
hear our prayers,
and help us to grow in the power of your Spirit,
through Jesus Christ our Saviour.

Amen.

Love God and your neighbour

Humbled by the wonder
of God's love for us all,
let us bring before him
our concerns.

We bring before him all Christians
who are troubled by doubt,
all who have lapsed from worshipping
or whose prayer time is threatened
by over-busy lives;
that they may know the nearness of Christ,
and be touched by his calm and stillness.
Silence
Father of all:
we come to you in love.

We bring before him the heated arguments,
industrial disputes,
blinkered vision and stubbornness
of our world;
that the power of God's love may soften,
ease and coax us all
to be more understanding,
wise and forgiving.
Silence
Father of all:
we come to you in love.

We bring before him widows,
widowers and orphans;
all broken families
and the socially rejected;
those who are disfigured or incapacitated;
that the warmth of God's love may radiate
all aspects of life, even the most painful,
to heal, comfort and transform.

Silence

Father of all:
we come to you in love.

We bring before him the areas of our own lives
which are in shadow and darkness;
that in the light of God's love
we may see our faults
and weaknesses more clearly
and notice the needs around us more readily,
so that in Christ's strength
we can show love in practical ways

Silence

Father of all:
we come to you in love.

Trustingly we pray to our loving Lord
for our own needs and cares.

Silence

Father,
we ask you to work your love in our lives,
and accept these prayers
we have brought to you,
through Jesus Christ our Lord.
Amen.

God's infinite kindness

United in the love of Christ,
let us unburden our needs and cares
to our heavenly Father.

We pray for all lapsed Christians;
all who have known him but rejected him;
all who doubt his love or are hesitant
to trust him with their lives;
that they may all be led back
to his welcoming arms.
Silence

Just as we are:
we come to you for help.

We pray for our world
with its blundering mistakes;
its weaknesses for self-indulgence and greed,
its misplaced affections
and well-meant interference;
that lives may be ordered and calmed
by the breath of his Spirit.
Silence

Just as we are:
we come to you for help.

We pray for all missing persons
and their families;
all who have lost their way emotionally
or professionally;

all whose minds are blurred or confused;
that all who are lost may be found,
and know the security
of being loved and protected
by their Creator.

Silence

Just as we are:
we come to you for help.

We pray for our own lives;
that they may be re-ordered,
calmed and refreshed by his Spirit,
and healed of all that shuts them off
from his love.

Silence

Just as we are:
we come to you for help.

God our Father knows our needs;
let us pray to him now
for our own intentions.

Silence

Father,
in thankful love
we ask you to hear our prayers,
for the sake of Jesus Christ.

Amen.

Christ renews
and transforms

Filled with hope
by our risen Lord,
let us pray to the Father
who has shown us such generous love.

We pray for the healing of divisions
among all who follow Christ;
that filled with hope by his resurrection
we may be inspired to break down barriers
to forgiveness and reconciliation.
Silence
Risen Lord Jesus:
transform our lives.

We pray for all who hold positions
of responsibility and leadership,
both internationally
and in our own community;
that they themselves may be led by God's Spirit
to make wise decisions
and help create a humane and caring world.
Silence
Risen Lord Jesus:
transform our lives.

We pray for all who incite others to antisocial,
addictive or criminal behaviour,

that they may be transformed and redirected;
for the weak, lonely, young and depressed,
who are so vulnerable to their temptations;
that they may be given help and strength
to resist the pressures around them.
Silence

Risen Lord Jesus:
transform our lives.

We pray for all families represented here;
their hopes and sorrows,
difficulties and celebrations;
that all our relationships
may be bathed in the love of Christ,
full of tenderness and compassion.
Silence

Risen Lord Jesus:
transform our lives.

In a time of silence,
we share with God our Father
our own personal burdens, joys and sorrows.
Silence

Father,
we bring you our cares and concerns,
and ask you to hear these prayers
through Jesus Christ our Lord.
Amen.

Christ gives new meaning to life

As members of the body of Christ,
let us pray to the Father
for the Church and for the world.

Let us pray for all Christian leaders
of all denominations;
for the healing of old wounds,
for forgiveness and an openness
to the Holy Spirit
who alone can make us one.
Silence
Lord of love:
teach us to care.

Let us pray for the areas
where there is poverty,
overcrowding and neglect;
for areas of depression
and high unemployment;
that, working hand in hand with God,
we may bring to the world the freshness
and vitality of hope
and caring love.
Silence
Lord of love:
teach us to care.

Let us pray for all who are trapped
by disability, illness or addiction,
all who feel unwanted or rejected;
that they may experience as a living reality
the liberation of Christ's accepting love.
Silence
Lord of love:
teach us to care.

Let us pray for the areas of our own lives
which need to be remade in Christ;
for any trying or difficult relationships,
anyone we tend to criticise or despise;
that God's uncompromising love
may inspire us to give without limits
and without exceptions.
Silence
Lord of love:
teach us to care.

In silence filled with love,
we name our particular prayer burdens.
Silence
Father,
we ask you to accept these prayers
through Jesus Christ,
and use us for your glory.
Amen.

Christ, the anointed King

Let us pray in the name of Christ,
who is here among us
and cares for us all.

We pray for the needs of his Church
as it works to reconcile humanity
with its Creator;
that Christians may speak
in words the world understands,
advising wisely, counselling lovingly
and welcoming wholeheartedly.
Silence
Christ, our King:
guide us in love.

We pray for the needs of each community
on this planet;
that wherever feelings have boiled over
and are out of control,
the calm reassurance of Christ
may restore harmony and goodwill.
Silence
Christ, our King:
guide us in love.

We pray for those attending hospitals and clinics,
those in residential homes;
for their relatives and friends,
and the staff who look after them;

that they may be sustained, strengthened,
and brought to wholeness
by the healing God of love.

Silence

Christ, our King:
guide us in love.

We pray for all who lead lonely, unhappy lives;
all whose marriages are crumbling;
all who cannot cope
with the demands of family life;
that as members of Christ
we may be shown where we can help,
and be given courage to act.

Silence

Christ, our King:
guide us in love.

We name in silence now
any known to us
with particular needs or burdens.

Silence

Loving Father,
we bring you these prayers
through Christ our Lord,
and through him we offer ourselves
to be used in your service.

Amen.

Worship, Discipleship, Mission

God wants mercy, not sacrifice

Let us pray to our heavenly Father
in thankfulness for his constant
love and loyalty,
bringing him our needs and concerns.

We pray for those involved in the planning
and leading of worship;
that all our worship
may be an outward expression
of deep, personal commitment
and never become careless
or empty repetition.

Silence

Father, hear us:
we know we can trust you.

We pray for those involved in welfare services,
prison management,
and those working in industry and commerce;
all whose work helps maintain peace and order;
that justice may always be administered with
   mercy,
and policies followed
which are grounded in loving care.

Silence

Father, hear us:
we know we can trust you.

We pray for all who have become
prisoners of habits,
whether drugs, self indulgence
or constant criticism;
that God may give us the power and confidence
to break those habits,
and that there may be mutual support
and encouragement
as we recognise our mutual
needs and weaknesses.
Silence
Father, hear us:
we know we can trust you.

We pray for our families, friends and neighbours;
that we may serve God in serving one another
cheerfully and ungrudgingly,
so that his kingdom of love and joy
may be established throughout the world.
Silence
Father, hear us:
we know we can trust you.

Trusting in God's loving mercy,
we pray in silence
for our own cares and concerns.
Silence
Father of mercy,
we rejoice at your welcoming forgiveness,
and ask you to accept our prayers
through Jesus Christ our Lord.
Amen.

Christ is our King

As fellow disciples of Christ,
let us ask God's blessing
on the Church and on the world.

We pray for the work
of Christ's body, the Church,
that all may labour zealously
for the establishment
of God's kingdom on earth
until the world is drenched
in his peace, joy and love.
Silence
God, our heavenly Father,
let your kingdom come.

We pray for the work
of all peacemakers and reformers;
all who work for justice,
reconciliation and harmony;
that the God of peace and love
will bless, support
and encourage them.
Silence
God, our heavenly Father,
let your kingdom come.

We pray for the work of those who heal and tend
the injured, sick and dying,
and those in their care;

for all involved in medical research
and those whose lives depend
on drugs, dialysis or radiotherapy.
Silence
God, our heavenly Father,
let your kingdom come.

We pray for our own work in this life;
that we may dedicate our energies
and resources more fully
to establishing Christ's kingdom;
that we may undertake every task
and activity joyfully
in the strength of our King.
Silence
God, our heavenly Father,
let your kingdom come.

In the warmth of God's love,
we pray in silence now
for our own particular concerns.
Silence
God our Father,
we ask you to accept our prayers,
through Jesus Christ our Lord.
Amen.

Endurance and reward

Let us lay at the feet
of God our Father
our needs and our cares,
as we pray together
in the Spirit of Jesus.

We lay at his feet
the need for ministry and leadership,
for a firm witness by all Christians
in the face of materialism and oppression;
for zeal and dedication among all members
of the body of Christ.

Silence

Lord, we trust you:
hold us safe in your hand.

We lay at his feet
the needs of our divided, fractious world;
its systems and schemes,
fashions and disasters;
that God's kingdom of love
may be established on earth,
as it is in heaven.

Silence

Lord, we trust you:
hold us safe in your hand.

We lay at his feet
the needs of all who suffer

in earthquakes, floods, droughts,
famine and epidemics;
all who try to supply relief
and medical aid;
that in Christ we may labour
for the good of the world.
Silence
Lord, we trust you:
hold us safe in your hand.

We lay at his feet
the needs of this community;
the local problems and injustices;
our Christian usefulness
in this corner of God's world.
Silence
Lord, we trust you:
hold us safe in your hand.

In silence, now,
we bring our private prayers to God
who knows what is in our hearts.
Silence
God our Father,
trusting in your constant care and protection,
we bring you these prayers
in the name of Jesus.
Amen.

Forgiven and forgiving

Let us pray at the feet
of God our Father
who loves us so dearly.

We pray for the spreading of the gospel
throughout all countries and cultures;
for all those working
to reconcile people
with their Creator;
for all involved in counselling
and spiritual teaching.
Silence

God, our loving Father:
make us worthy of our calling.

We pray for a deepening spirit
of fellowship and goodwill
among the people of this earth;
for a greater willingness to forgive,
negotiate, communicate and support.
Silence

God, our loving Father:
make us worthy of our calling.

We pray for all victims
of violence and aggression;
for those obsessed with hatred
and retaliation;
for the injured, abused

and the dying.

Silence

God, our loving Father:
make us worthy of our calling.

We pray for God's guidance and restoration
in our own lives;
for more awareness of our faults
and areas of blindness;
for a greater understanding
of God's love for us.

Silence

God, our loving Father:
make us worthy of our calling.

In silence, now,
we pour out to God our Father
any needs and burdens
known to us personally.

Silence

Heavenly Father,
trusting in your amazing love,
we ask you to accept these prayers,
through Jesus Christ our Lord.

Amen.

Persevere in prayer

Let us quieten our hearts
in the presence of the unchanging
and everlasting Father,
and pray.

We pray for all those involved
in the ceaseless praying
on our spinning earth;
for all contemplative orders,
and those whose lives
are rooted in prayer;
for those learning to pray
and those who feel they cannot pray.
Silence
Spirit of Jesus:
live in our hearts and minds.

We pray for the world,
for victory of good over evil
in every situation
whether of international
or local significance;
for a deepening of trust
and a desire for truth and peace.

Silence
Spirit of Jesus:
live in our hearts and minds.

We pray for the disheartened and uninspired;
for those whose lives are frustrating
and endlessly stressful;
for the homeless
and the unemployed;
and for those addicted to drugs,
alcohol or gambling.

Silence

Spirit of Jesus:
live in our hearts and minds.

We pray for the members of our own families,
with their particular needs,
for our local shopkeepers, teachers,
doctors, nurses,
and all who work in this area.

Silence

Spirit of Jesus:
live in our hearts and minds.

In silence, we bring our own prayers
to God our Father,
who knows all our needs.

Silence

God, our heavenly Father,
bless our lives to your service,
and accept our prayers,
through Jesus Christ our Lord.

Amen.

May God's kingdom come

As friends in Christ,
and in the stillness of his peace,
let us pray together.

We pray for all those involved
with missionary work
both abroad and at home;
that they may be protected
from danger and disease,
and led in the way of God's will,
so that their caring, forgiving lives
witness to his love.
Silence

Take us, remake us:
and let your kingdom come.

We pray for all the peoples of this earth
who do not know God;
for those who see him only as a threat
or an excuse for violence;
that they may be brought into contact
with the living Christ
who longs to give them his peace.
Silence

Take us, remake us:
and let your kingdom come.

We pray for those in physical or mental pain;
those weakened and exhausted by illness,

those in intensive care
or undergoing emergency surgery;
that God's healing power
will sustain them
and make them whole.
Silence
Take us, remake us:
and let your kingdom come.

We pray for those with whom we live
and work and worship;
that we may use every opportunity
to care for each other
and grow in patience
and understanding.
Silence
Take us, remake us:
and let your kingdom come.

Confident in God's welcoming love,
we pray in silence now
for our own particular needs and concerns.
Silence
God our Father,
accept these prayers,
in Jesus' name we ask.
Amen.

Costly grace

Remembering our dependence
on God for all things,
let us pray to the Lord.

We pray for those whose Christian witness
has brought embarrassment,
rejection or persecution;
that with their sights fixed on Jesus,
Christians may be strengthened and encouraged,
and remain his faithful friends.
Silence
Hear us, Father:
you are our strength and joy.

We pray for all negotiators, diplomats,
envoys and advisers;
that they may seek peace
rather than war,
unity rather than division,
and justice
rather than personal success.
Silence
Hear us, Father:
you are our strength and joy.

We pray that the healing love of God
may work within those
who have been discouraged or hurt;
all who harbour resentment

and the desire for revenge;
the lonely, the timid,
the vulnerable and the abused.
Silence
Hear us, Father:
you are our strength and joy.

We pray for our local community
and all its homes, shops,
schools, surgeries and leisure facilities;
that we, as Christians,
may bring Christ's life and brightness
to this place
so that it is infused with his love.
Silence
Hear us, Father:
you are our strength and joy.

Trustingly, we pray in silence
to God our Father,
who considers each one of us special.
Silence
Loving Father,
hear our prayers,
through Jesus Christ our Lord.
Amen.

Praying to the Father

As we have been invited to do,
we pray to our heavenly Father.

We pray for the continuous worship of the Church
in every different climate,
culture and season;
that the waves of constant praise
and thanksgiving
may never be broken;
that Christians may pray attentively,
joyfully and faithfully.
Silence
Our Father in heaven:
may your kingdom come.

We pray for those in positions of authority;
that they may neither abuse their power
nor ignore their responsibilities
but act with integrity, compassion
and generosity of spirit.
Silence
Our Father in heaven:
may your kingdom come.

We pray for all families split
by political boundaries,
war or natural disasters;
for all who have nowhere
to call their home,

and those for whom no one cares
or prays.
Silence
Our Father in heaven:
may your kingdom come.

We pray for our own parents,
for family life
throughout the whole world;
that all homes may be blessed
with love and security
and reflect God's love
for his children.
Silence
Our Father in heaven:
may your kingdom come.

In silence filled with love,
we name our particular prayer burdens.
Silence
God our Father,
rejoicing in your tenderness and compassion,
we bring these prayers before you
through Jesus Christ our Lord.
Amen.

Good News of eternal life

As children of our heavenly Father,
let us quieten ourselves and pray.

We pray for the Church,
that having led others,
Christians may not themselves
be found wanting;
that they may be open
to what Christ needs them to do.

Silence

Lord, I believe:
help my unbelief.

We pray for our busy, rushed
and anxious world;
for those weighed down
with responsibilities,
and for the daily routine
of millions of individuals
on this earth;
that God's Good News
may bring to each separate person
life in all its abundance.

Silence

Lord, I believe:
help my unbelief.

We pray for those who profess to believe,
but whose lives are dark and joyless;

that they may experience the
welcoming love of Christ
and be drawn more fully
into his resurrection life.

Silence

Lord, I believe:
help my unbelief.

We pray for ourselves and our families;
that we may not waste our life on earth
pursuing futile goals,
but commit ourselves absolutely
to following Christ,
who has power to save us.

Silence

Lord, I believe:
help my unbelief.

In silence,
we bring our individual prayers
to the Lord of all.

Silence

Heavenly Father,
we ask you to hear our prayers,
in the name of our Lord and Saviour,
Jesus Christ.

Amen.

Unchanging Father

Let us quieten our hearts
to listen to the Lord of peace,
and to pray to him.

We pray for all Christians
involved in teaching and nursing,
and those who have chosen
to live simple lives;
for the growth and development
of a strong prayer life
in every Christian.
Silence
Unchanging Father:
give us your peace.

We pray for the world of industry
and commerce;
for those whose decisions
affect many lives;
for those who determine the use
of our world's resources.
Silence
Unchanging Father:
give us your peace.

We pray for those who are suffering
from stress and depression;
for psychiatric nursing staff;
for those who cannot cope

with the burdens of their lives.
Silence
Unchanging Father:
give us your peace.

We pray for ourselves and our families;
for a greater simplicity
in the ordering of our lives;
for deeper trust and acceptance.
Silence
Unchanging Father:
give us your peace.

Upheld by God's peace,
we pray now in silence
for any needs known to us personally.
Silence
Heavenly Father,
accept our prayers,
through Jesus Christ our Lord.
Amen.

Christ, our Saviour, is here

Gathered in the presence of Christ,
let us pray.

We pray that the Church may worship and adore
faithfully and courageously
in every age,
coming to know Christ
more and more.

Silence

Hear us, Father:
make your will ours.

We pray that the world may recognise
and believe
that Jesus is truly
the Son of God.

Silence

Hear us, Father:
make your will ours.

We pray that all those in physical,
mental, emotional or spiritual need
may be comforted.

Silence

Hear us, Father:
make your will ours.

We pray that in celebrating our faith
we may be sensitive
to one another's needs,
kind, helpful
and full of gratitude.

Silence

Hear us, Father:
make your will ours.

We pray in silence, now,
for our own particular
needs and concerns.

Silence

Heavenly Father,
accept these prayers
and give us the strength and the will
to walk in love,
through Jesus Christ our Lord.

Amen.

Facing hardship

As children of our heavenly Father,
let us approach him
with our needs and cares.

We bring the problems of communication
in the Church, and in all church groups;
the difficulties of finding
enough church leaders, cleaners,
teachers, visitors
to work effectively for God
in our area.
Silence
Loving heavenly Father:
guide us in your love.

We bring the pressures
on those in business
to think only in terms
of what is profitable;
the problems of wealth distribution
which cause unnecessary suffering
in our world.
Silence
Loving heavenly Father:
guide us in your love.

We bring the shortage of staff
and resources in hospitals;
the distress of those

who have no hospital to go to;
the suffering of those
who are in physical pain,
mental anguish or spiritual darkness.
Silence

Loving heavenly Father:
guide us in your love.

We bring the things that irritate,
anger and frustrate us;
the jobs that we find difficult to do cheerfully;
the relationships we find demanding and tiring.
Silence

Loving heavenly Father:
guide us in your love.

Trustingly, we pray in silence
to our loving Lord,
who considers each one of us special.
Silence

Father,
you always give us far more
than we can ever deserve;
please fulfil our prayers
in the way that is best for us.
We ask in the name of Jesus Christ.
Amen.

Jesus is Lord in all circumstances

Let us pour out to our loving heavenly Father
the areas of need and concern
in the Church and in our world.

We commend to our loving Father
all who persist in working
to spread the news
of Christ's saving love
in spite of poor conditions,
hostility or danger.
Silence

Lord of our strength:
with you all things are possible.

We commend to our loving Father
all who have been elected to govern
both locally and internationally;
that being guided by the light
of truth and goodness
they may be good stewards
of the resources in their care.
Silence

Lord of our strength:
with you all things are possible.

We commend to our loving Father
the chronically and critically ill,

and those who tend them;
the babies being born today,
and the people who will die today.
Silence
Lord of our strength:
with you all things are possible.

We commend to our loving Father
those we love who do not yet know Christ,
or have turned away from him;
that through circumstances
and relationships
they may be drawn to seek him.
Silence
Lord of our strength:
with you all things are possible.

In the knowledge
that God our Father hears us,
let us offer
our own particular prayers.
Silence
Father of mercy,
hear our prayers
which we offer through Jesus Christ.
Amen.

Obedience to Christ

We have been drawn here today
by the power of God's love;
into that love let us now gather
all those for whom we pray.

We commend to his love
all who are working for Christian unity;
that their work may be guided and blessed
with integrity, wisdom and purity.
Silence

Father, almighty;
let your will be done.

We commend to his love
all judges, and those serving on juries;
those who make laws in our own country
and throughout the world;
that our human laws may reflect
the unchanging law and will
of the God we know in Christ.
Silence

Father, almighty;
let your will be done.

We commend to his love
those whose minds have been poisoned
by exposure to violence;
children who have been abandoned
or maltreated;

all who crave affection
but are frightened
to become emotionally involved
in case they get hurt.

Silence

Father, almighty;
let your will be done.

We commend to his love
our own areas of weakness;
that we may be remade by God's grace
into the sort of people
he desires us to be.

Silence

Father, almighty;
let your will be done.

As God's stillness fills our hearts,
we pray for our own particular needs
and concerns.

Silence

Heavenly Father,
in your love and mercy hear our prayers,
through Jesus Christ our Lord.

Amen.

The challenge of faith

United in his Spirit,
let us pray to our heavenly Father.

We pray that all Christian people
may proclaim the full truth
about Jesus Christ,
without dilution or distortion,
even though that truth
may sometimes be unpalatable.
Silence
Bountiful Father:
give us your grace.

We pray that we may be
wise and careful stewards
of the resources of our world,
so as to live out our thankfulness.
Silence
Bountiful Father:
give us your grace.

We pray that those who are physically hungry
may be fed;
and those who hunger and thirst
for real meaning in life
may be led to find lasting nourishment
in Jesus.

Silence
Bountiful Father:
give us your grace.

We pray that having received Christ
into our hearts,
we may joyfully,
in words and actions,
spread the marvellous news of his saving love.
Silence
Bountiful Father:
give us your grace.

Meeting our heavenly Father
in the stillness of silence,
let us bring to him
our own particular cares and concerns.
Silence
Father,
we can never thank you enough
for what you have done for us,
and for the way you are transforming our lives;
with grateful hearts we offer you these prayers
in the name of Jesus.
Amen.

Working for God's glory

We are God's children,
and he loves us;
let us pray to him now.

We bring to his love
those whose Christian ministry
is in prisons, hospitals,
schools or industry;
those who work among the homeless
and the very poor.
Silence
Father, you have called us:
let our lives show your glory.

We bring to his love
the areas of political tension
and unrest in our world;
the unresolved conflicts
and the deep seated grudges
that hinder peace.
Silence
Father, you have called us:
let our lives show your glory.

We bring to his love
the hurt and wounded,
the abused and the frightened;
women in labour and newly born babies;
those who are approaching death.

Silence
Father, you have called us:
let our lives show your glory.

We bring to his love the needs
of those who live or work in this area,
and any who have particularly
asked for our prayers.
(mention these by name)
Silence

Father, you have called us:
let our lives show your glory.

In silence, now,
we bring to God's love
the special needs and concerns
known to us individually.
Silence

With special joy, Father,
in the knowledge
that we can trust you unconditionally,
we offer you our prayers,
through Jesus Christ.
Amen.

Trust God and fear not

Together we walk the way of Christ;
let us now pray together in his name,
to our Lord and heavenly Father.

We pray that the spiritual life
of each church community
may be nurtured and grow,
so that Christians may have confidence
to reach out increasingly
to the particular needs
of their neighbourhood.
Silence

Lord, we trust you:
let us faithfully serve.

We pray that God's will may prevail
in the way we use our world's resources,
our intelligence,
our knowledge
and our power.
Silence

Lord, we trust you:
let us faithfully serve.

We pray that all those
who are living through some tempest,
whether physical, emotional,
mental or spiritual,
may know the peace and comfort
of God's absorbent love

which soaks up all hurt
and promotes healing and wholeness.
Silence
Lord, we trust you:
let us faithfully serve.

We pray that our homes may be havens
of caring and understanding,
where all who enter may find
the tangible and attractive peace
of the God we serve.
Silence
Lord, we trust you:
let us faithfully serve.

Trusting in God our Father,
we name our particular prayer burdens.
Silence
Father,
rejoicing that you are
in overall charge of all creation,
we offer these prayers
through Jesus Christ.
Amen.

Rooted in Christ

As members of the body of Christ,
full of thankfulness for his abiding love,
let us pray to our heavenly Father
who knows us so well.

Let us ask God to deepen
the personal commitment
of every Christian,
so that the life-giving sap
of the true vine
can flood through the Church
and out into the world.
Silence

Let your life be in us, Father:
that we may bear fruit.

Let us ask God to direct and further
all international discussions
so that they lead to peace,
goodwill and greater understanding.
Silence

Let your life be in us, Father:
that we may bear fruit.

Let us ask God to bring healing
to those who are ill,
peace to the anxious,
courage to the fearful
and rest to the weary.

Silence

Let your life be in us, Father:
that we may bear fruit.

Let us ask God to make his home in us,
in our marriages and our homes,
our places of work
and in our local community,
so that our characters can be forged
by his Spirit in us.

Silence

Let your life be in us, Father:
that we may bear fruit.

Confident in God's life-giving love,
we pray in silence now
for our individual needs.

Silence

Merciful Father,
fulfil our needs
according to your loving wisdom,
through Jesus Christ.

Amen.

The light of Christ is revealed

Let us pray together
for the Church
and for the world.

We pray that our Christian witness
in a confused and nervous world
may shine with a piercing integrity
and warmth
that awakens people's hearts
to the love of their Creator.
Silence
Light of the nations:
shine in our lives.

We pray that all travellers and pilgrims
may be blessed and protected;
that we may learn to cherish the beauty
of our world
and share its riches.
Silence
Light of the nations:
shine in our lives.

We pray that we may be directed to seek
the best practical ways
of providing shelter for the homeless,
safe accommodation for those

who live in fear of violence,
and food for the hungry.
Silence
Light of the nations:
shine in our lives.

We pray that we may learn to see Christ
in the eyes of all those we meet,
and delight in giving God glory
by serving others
without expecting rewards.
Silence
Light of the nations:
shine in our lives.

Knowing that God our Father is listening,
we bring our personal prayers to him now.
Silence
In thankfulness, Father,
we offer you our lives
and our prayers,
through Jesus Christ.
Amen.

INDEX

Lightning Source UK Ltd.
Milton Keynes UK
29 August 2009

143184UK00001B/7/P

9 780862 098537